COMMUNICATION AND LEARNING IN
SMALL GROUPS

Routledge Direct Editions

COMMUNICATION AND LEARNING IN SMALL GROUPS

DOUGLAS BARNES
School of Education, University of Leeds

and

FRANKIE TODD
Department of Contemporary Studies, Leeds Polytechnic

ROUTLEDGE DIRECT EDITIONS

ROUTLEDGE & KEGAN PAUL
London, Henley and Boston

First published in 1977
by Routledge & Kegan Paul Ltd
39 Store Street,
London WC1E 7DD,
Broadway House,
Newtown Road,
Henley-on-Thames,
Oxon RG9 1EN and
9 Park Street,
Boston, Mass. 02108, USA
Manuscript typed by Alice Rockwell
Printed and bound in Great Britain
by Unwin Brothers Limited,
The Gresham Press, Old Woking, Surrey
A member of the Staples Printing Group

ISBN 0 7100 8512 5

CONTENTS

ACKNOWLEDGMENTS

The work that follows arose from a project funded by the Social
Science Research Council and based at the University of Leeds
Institute of Education. We are glad to acknowledge the support
given by both of these institutions. We should also like to thank
a number of other people who gave us help during the project's life.

First of these must be the headmasters, teachers and pupils of
John Smeaton High School and Foxwood High School, both of Leeds.
The teachers who worked with us readily gave substantial amounts of
time in planning tasks and organising recording sessions, and the
children too were most helpful and pleasant to work with. Without
this co-operation the research could not have been done.

We gained many insights from discussions with members of the
CLSG Seminar Groups which met at the University of Leeds regularly
throughout the project's life. We are especially grateful to
Martin Hammersley, now of the Open University, for the part he
played in crystallising the views expressed in Chapter 4 - although
he may not entirely agree with our present position.

Finally, we should like to thank Mrs Connie Langton, the
project's secretary, for her careful work on the transcriptions, her
general support throughout the life of the project, and especially
for her efforts to enable us to complete the Final Report to the
SSRC on time.

INTRODUCTION

This is a study of the talk of thirteen-year-old boys and girls, recorded while they were working in small groups on tasks which their teachers had set. When we played back the recordings to the teachers, their reactions were commonly of surprise and delight. They were surprised because the quality of the children's discussions typically far exceeded the calibre of their contributions in class; and were pleased to hear the children manifesting unexpected skills and competences.

This surprise seems to be linked to teachers' assumptions about what pupils can do. Many notions of schooling present pupils as passive receivers of learning. Teachers know, but pupils do not; if they do, they know imperfectly. More importantly, it seems to be often assumed that if children are to approach a deeper knowledge, or to increase their understanding, this will only be possible under the direct guidance and control of the teacher. However, in analysing recordings of groups of children working alone, we came to the conclusion that, under certain circumstances at least, children are able to talk to good purpose, and to increase their understanding, without calling on adult resources. In saying this, it is crucial to note that we are not denying the importance and necessity of the teacher, nor are we arguing that small group methods are necessarily a good thing in themselves. We do believe, however, that children are often underestimated, and that they possess skills and competences which are rarely called upon in a conventional classroom. And this is where the importance of small group discussion lies, for it is only in this situation that many of these skills are manifested. If they are not drawn on in class, it follows that the teacher may never know that these skills exist.

Work on interaction in the classroom indicates that in class discussion it is the teacher who manages and controls the discourse. Not only do teachers do most of the talking, but they also take responsibility for the content, pacing and style of pupil contributions. Teachers decide the topic for discussion, nominate some pupils to speak, hush other pupils, and judge the relevance of pupil contributions. When children are talking in a group without an adult present, responsibility for the management of the talk falls on themselves. They must negotiate who talks, when, and how. They X must cope with occasional episodes of conflict, and with silences. They must encourage group members with useful contributions to make, and at the same time, control any attempts to dominate the talk for irrelevant purposes. They must judge the relevance of contributions, and monitor whether they are germane to the problem set; they must also maintain some overall judgment of the quality of the discussion, so as to assess when they have reached a point where it is reasonable to stop.

Not surprisingly, the groups whose talk we recorded varied in the extent to which they were successful in coping with these demands. But none of them fulfilled the gloomy forecasts of giggling, playing about, or refusing even to attempt the task. All of the groups tried to do the work which was set them; and enough of the groups produced talk of sufficiently high calibre for us to want to document and describe it.

The first chapter describes the children and the contexts in which the recordings were made, and discusses ways of analysing talk, and some of the difficulties which we met in attempting this. In the second chapter we illustrate and discuss in detail the strengths - and occasional weaknesses - shown by the children in their talk. Chapter 3 is particularly addressed to teachers who wish to use and to study small group talk in their own teaching. The last two chapters are more theoretical and are concerned with the nature of meaning in conversations.

Chapter 1

THE CHILDREN AND THEIR TALK

1 PURPOSES OF THE STUDY

Reports of research commonly present 'findings', which represent
aspects of the final state of understanding reached by the researchers. This necessarily excludes an account of lines of
thought, enquiry, or analysis, which at an earlier stage of the
research seemed promising, but which later proved abortive. Nevertheless, a description of some of these dead-ends may prove informative. For this reason we propose to present not merely a version
of our present understanding but an account of how we reached this
state. This report therefore begins with an account of how we saw
the task ahead of us when we began.
    It is a commonplace that there are relationships between what is
known and the social location of the knower. Much of the discussion
of these relationships has been concerned with large-scale social
factors such as social class. The underlying purpose of this study
was to examine the relationship between short-term, small-scale
aspects of the social interaction of small groups and the cognitive
strategies generated in the course of this interaction. We expected it to be possible to carry out concurrent analyses of social
interaction and cognitive strategies (whatever these were) as they
appeared within the acts of communication themselves. Education
provides a social context set up primarily for the control of
knowledge by the patterning of communication. Small groups were
chosen in order to obtain as much information as possible about the
learning strategies of children in the absence of a teacher.
    In planning this study we were making a number of assumptions
about cognition and its relationship to speech. First, we assumed
(and continue to assume) that speech functions as a means by which
people construct and reconstruct views of the world about them,
often jointly, when the speech is a means of communicating with
other people. Thus we set out to investigate the interplay between
cognitive and communicative functions of speech in contexts planned
for learning.
    Our second group of assumptions related to an aspect of this
interplay. We assumed that one of the means by which adolescents
achieve hypothetico-deductive thinking (formal operations) is

1

through internalising the viewpoints of other people, and that this internalisation takes place in the course of dialogues in which different viewpoints are interrelated through verbal interaction with other people. We hoped to be able to describe those features of a dialogue through which participants encouraged (or discouraged) one another to articulate and interrelate their points of view.

We expected that the way in which language was used would be affected by (a) the learners, (b) the subject-matter, (c) the demands laid upon the learners (these two together constituting 'the task'), and (d) the social situation in which the learning took place. These will now be discussed in turn.

We chose to work with thirteen-year-olds of average ability since research done by Piaget and his associates indicates that the thinking of such children will be mainly at the intuitive level (concrete operations), only rising occasionally under specially helpful conditions to hypothetico-deductive modes of thinking. We hoped that this would enable us more readily to investigate the effect of variations in task and situation upon the mode of thinking used, and also to trace in the dialogue those strategies which encouraged or impeded hypothetico-deductive thinking. We planned to work with children of average intelligence from relatively homogeneous backgrounds, since intelligence and social class were not the variables which we wished to investigate.

Since subject-matter must exert an influence on discussion, we chose to work with teachers of several different subjects. In collaboration with them we constructed problem-like tasks which were derived from work which children were doing in class and which we judged to be amenable to small group discussion. We originally intended to limit the range of tasks to five types: the interpretation of verbal evidence; the interpretation of apparatus, maps or pictures; the reorganising of existing knowledge in order to apply it to new problems; the planning of methods for testing hypotheses; the planning of displays of knowledge in new form. In fact these types proved not to have a realistic relationship to the topics proposed by the teachers we were working with; most of the tasks eventually chosen overlapped into more than one of these types, and often contained other elements also.

We expected that the nature of group talk would be influenced by a wide and complex system of situational variables. We chose three of these as likely to be particularly relevant to classroom learning: (a) the tightness with which the teacher structures the task and the terms of reference within which it would be performed; (b) the pupils' expectations about the reception of their results, especially whether they are to be reported to their teacher and criticised by him; (c) the level of familiarity existing between participants, including any adults present. (At the same time, the expectations brought by the children to the recording sessions must radically affect the communication which occurs, thus modifying the effects of task and situational variables.)

This line of thought had arisen from a small study (1) carried out by one of the authors, which had raised questions and hypotheses related to (a) hypothetical modes of speech, (b) collaboration between group members during problem-solving, and (c) the effect of giving increased control of learning to the learners. It is ap-

propriate at this stage to make some of these hypotheses and
questions explicit.

We expected that it would be possible to place group talk along
a dimension running from intimate to public. We thought that small
groups' talk - in contrast to most talk in traditional lessons -
would fall at the 'intimate' end of the scale, and that problem-
solving in an 'intimate' group would have characteristics that might
be called 'exploratory'. These exploratory characteristics would
include: hesitations and changes of direction; tentativeness shown
in intonation; assertions and questions in the hypothetical modality, inviting modification and surmise; self-monitoring and reflexivity.

A second characteristic that interested us was the level of 'collaborativeness' in a group's approach to the task. This collaborativeness might be shown in their talk by markers such as these:
close links between succeeding utterances, including frequent modifications or extension of a preceding remark; frequent questions,
especially those asking for further expansion of a contribution;
self-awareness in approaching the task, including deliberate control
of the discussion by recapitulation, restatement of the task, and
the explicit interrelation of viewpoints. We expected collaborativeness also to be characterised by attentiveness to the social
needs of others, and by a low level of competition for the right to
speak. To sum up, collaboration was thought to depend upon (a)
invitation to others to participate, (b) extension of previous
contributions, and (c) acknowledgment of others' identities.

In moving control over learning strategies into the learner's
hands (in contrast to a teacher's control) we expected to be able
to show that a wider range of speech roles was available to the
learner; and that these would include hypothesis-forming and testing, and the ability to go beyond the given information and to
generate new questions and tasks.

We wished to develop a method of analysis which would include the
various markers which have been mentioned above, and which therefore
would allow our implicit hypotheses about collaboration and exploratory talk to be tested empirically. We hoped to achieve a
sequential analysis since it seemed unlikely that an analysis into a
set of categories would be appropriate to the phenomena we wished to
describe. Our analysis must include both cognitive and interactive
aspects.

In analysing interaction we hoped to develop a system which would
display for each utterance (a) how it related to foregoing utterances, (b) a 'level of modality' which would be a measure of its
position on a tentative-dogmatic dimension (c) the speech-role being
adopted (d) indication of some verbal forms which carried out these
functions. This display was to incorporate the markers referred to
above in discussing 'the exploratory mode', 'collaborativeness', and
the effects of learners' control. Alongside this analysis we
intended to assign each utterance to a 'cognitive level', according
to a scheme to be based on Piaget's developmental sequence.

This completes the account of the intentions with which we set
out on this study. In the event, some of these intentions were not
put into effect, and other purposes and methods were taken up in the
course of our work. These are described in the remainder of this
chapter.

2   THE CHILDREN AND THE CONTEXT

Over a period of twelve months, beginning in January 1973, we made
recordings of secondary school children talking in small groups,
without a teacher being present. Altogether we have about 11 hours
of such discussions, in which a total of 56 children participated.
We worked in two large upper schools, each with a predominantly
white working class intake. These were schools where we had been
offered substantial co-operation from the teachers; for instance,
teachers were willing to allow us to withdraw small groups of
children from lessons so that we could record them, and they also
helped us to make up tasks for the children to work on. Our data
collection was carried out in two main phases (which are summarised
in Table 1).

First phase of data collection

The first phase of recordings were carried out at two schools,
which we refer to as Schools X and Y. From each school's third
year, we selected eight boys and eight girls of average ability.
We began at School X, a large unstreamed upper school on the edge
of countryside, flanked on the city side by council-housing estates.
We made our first set of recordings here over a period of six
months, during which we visited the school very frequently. Conse-
quently, we got to know the sixteen children involved (Groups 1-4)
very well, and to have a friendly relationship with them. During
this period we were making approaches to other schools, trying to
find another suitable one to co-operate with us. This search took
some time, so we were not able to begin recording in School Y until
some months later. This was another large comprehensive, neither
'inner-city' nor 'suburban', but somewhere in between, again with a
predominantly white working-class intake. Here were recorded a
further sixteen children (Groups 5-8) during about two months.
    The recordings made at these two schools provided us with our
initial set of data. Altogether, these comprised 29 discussions,
made by 32 children on 9 topics. In this first set of recordings,
the children worked in groups of four, each made up of two boys and
two girls.

Selection of children

An overriding criterion in the selection of children to take part
was that they had to be taught by all the teachers who were working
with us. This limited us to one class at each school. Additionally, we wanted to work with 'average' rather than either very bright
or very dull children. We decided to exclude very bright children
on the grounds that we wanted any ultimate recommendations we might
make to be applicable to teachers working with ordinary children,
rather than only to those who work with brighter children. We excluded very dull children because we thought it likely they would
neither produce a sufficient volume of talk to be analysable, nor
be able to read and understand the task card's directions. We used

TABLE 1 The groups and their tasks

FIRST PHASE DATA COLLECTION

School X (5¼ hrs)

	'The Pearl' (Jan. 73)	'National Parks' (Jan. 73)	'Causes of Vandalism' (Jan. 73)	'Work/ Energy' (Feb. 73)	'Steve's Letter' (March 73)	'Carbon Dioxide in Water' (March 73)	'Dis- cussions' (June 73)
Group 1	1	1	1	1	–	–	1
Group 2	2	2	–	2	–	–	2
Group 3	3	3	3	–	–	–	3
Group 4	4	4	4	4	4	–	4
(mixed) Group X	–	–	–	–	–	X	–
(mixed) Group Y	–	–	–	–	–	Y	–

FIRST PHASE DATA COLLECTION

School Y (2 hrs)

	'Life in Trenches' (March 73)	'Bird's Eggs' (June 73)
Group 5	5	5
Group 6	6	6
Group 7	7	7
Group 8	8	8

SECOND PHASE DATA COLLECTION

School X (3¾ hrs)

	'Spaceman' (Jan. 74)	'Gang Violence' (Jan. 74)
(Girls) Group 9	9 Assess	9 Non-Assess
(Girls) Group 10	10 Non-Assess	10 Assess
(Girls) Group 11	11 Assess	11 Non-Assess
(Girls) Group 12	12 Non-Assess	12 Assess
(Boys) Group 13	13 Non-Assess	
(Boys) Group 14	14 Assess	14 Non-Assess
(Boys) Group 15	15 Non-Assess	15 Assess
(Boys) Group 16	16 Assess	16 Non-Assess

the teachers' ratings of the children's abilities, plus school
records, to select children of average ability. Since the children
all came from one class, they all knew each other quite well. In
so far as compatible with grouping two boys and two girls together,
the groups we put the children to work in approximated to what the
teachers thought were their existing friendship groups.

The tasks

The topics that we asked the children to work on were all based on
work being covered in class; they were drawn from subject areas
across the curriculum, including Social Studies, English, Physics,
Biology, History, and Geography. We asked each of the teachers who
worked with us to let us know when they were going to cover a topic
that could be used for small group work. We then collaborated with
the teachers in the construction of a 'task card' - a card with the
task typed on it - that was based on this class-work. Sometimes
the tasks were quite open, but more often they were made up of a
set of directions for procedures to be gone through, questions to
be covered in a certain order, and so on. Some Science tasks involved manipulation of apparatus, and some Humanities and English
tasks had materials to be worked on, such as the text of an interview.

Task situation and procedure

It is important to note that the children were not required to approach any of these topics 'cold'. In each case, before they came
to record with us, they had done some work on the topic in class,
with their teacher. Before they did any recording at all, before
they even met us, the children at School X were given an overall
account of what we were trying to do by one of their teachers, and
they were given a general outline of what participation in our
project would involve. We believe that these two kinds of preparation had a marked influence on the characteristics and quality of
the resulting discussions. We withdrew 'our' children from class
time to record them. This gained for us excellent recordings and
relatively detailed transcriptions, but may have made the talk less
like pupil-talk in group-work in class.
     There were differences between the two schools in terms of the
children's familiarity with the experience of small group work, and
also their prior experience with tape recorders. School X seemed
to use group work as a matter of course, so the children were familiar with working in this way. (However, it is worth noting that
the teachers' and the children's accounts were discrepant: the
children said they did not do much work in groups, and the teachers
thought they did quite a lot.) Many of these children possessed
tape recorders of their own, and taping their own talk had already
played a part in some lessons, so they were relatively sophisticated about being recorded. At School Y, small group work seemed
to be used rarely if at all, so this was not a context with which
the children were familiar. Being tape recorded seemed also to be

a novel and somewhat worrying experience. The children at this
school did not get a preliminary presentation of our aims from a
teacher either. These three differences show in the differences
between the talk of these children and the talk of children from
School X.

On the first occasion that the children came to be recorded, we
carried out a fairly standard procedure aimed at minimising microphone shyness. We chatted to them for a while before moving on to
the research task, and we recorded some of this conversation and
played it back to the children to give them a chance to talk about
how they felt about the sound of their own voices. We always made
sure that the investigator was recorded too, so that this experience
was shared with the children. Most of the children did not like the
sound of their own voices, or found it very strange, so we discussed
with them the ways in which the parameters of the sound recording
and playback system tended to distort features of the voice's pitch
and timbre. And the investigator would admit that his/her recorded
voice had sounded strange at first, but that with familiarity this
was something to which one became accustomed. Also at this first
meeting we gave the children an explanation of the project's overall
interests, explained to them what we would be asking them to do, and
answered any questions raised. On subsequent occasions, we cut out
the preliminary recording, and the overall account of the project,
but we always made time for general social chat before asking the
children to do the task.

On all occasions, we read out the task card slowly to the
children (each child had a copy), asked them to discuss it, and told
them to switch the tape recorder off when they had finished. Then
the investigator left the room until called in by the children when
they felt they had done enough talking.

Children's control of the tape-recorder

We should perhaps emphasise that we gave the children themselves
considerable control over the recording situation. No one was in
the room with them when they talked, they could decide for themselves when to stop talking, and they could also switch the tape
recorder off whenever they liked. (We showed them how to do this.)
They used this facility at first to maintain privacy when they
wanted to say something which they thought was not suitable for our
ears. As they got to know us better, there was a decrease in the
number of occasions when they switched the recorder off for a short
period (this made an audible 'click' on the tape), and instead they
would lower their voices to whisper. In practice, we could transcribe most of these whispers, so we know that the talk that they
didn't intend to share with us was often concerned with planning
what to do next, with mentioning ongoing events briefly, or, very
occasionally, with the exchange of insults. As time went on, the
groups we had most contact with stopped bothering even to lower
their voices, so the social tone of the recordings became increasingly uninhibited.

In time, they learned how to rewind the tape and play back
sections of their talk to themselves. We did not expressly show

them how to do this (although of course we carried out the relevant operations in front of them time and time again), but we never expressed any disapproval of it. In any case groups did not spend too much of their time doing this. We gave the children this amount of control over the context they were working in because we wanted to make the work in groups a joint venture which they shared with us, rather than something that was imposed on them from the top. One might query what there was for them to share: the researcher's gratifications are visible enough, but what reward do his subjects get out of the research situation? One reward we were able to give them was the chance to hear what they sounded like in ordinary conversation. At the end of the group's work, the investigator always offered to play back to them a lengthy section from their talk. The children welcomed this, and appeared to get pleasure from it. The session usually ended amid jokes and laughter, and also some serious evaluative comments about the work they had just done. Often during this relaxed period the children would ask further questions about the aims of the project and there would follow some discussion of why we were doing it and why we had become interested in this area. All of this seemed to help to make the enterprise something that was shared between ourselves and the children, something that was rewarding to them as well as to us.

Second phase of data collection

The data collection during our first phase of recordings was meant (a) to be a pilot run for something more controlled in the future, and (b) to provide data from which we could construct an analytical system, which would be used to analyse further data to be collected in a more controlled way at a later stage. Initially, we had intended that the second phase of data collection would be in the form of a classic experimental design, involving statistical treatment to test the effects of (i) kinds of task and (ii) the expectation of being assessed by a teacher, on the forms of the communication within the groups.

However, during the course of the first year's work, we had already begun to run into some unanticipated problems, which indicated that a classic experimental study might be impossible - and inappropriate if it were possible.

One problem was that we had great difficulty developing an analytical system that seemed to be even moderately reliable, inclusive, and also meaningful. (It would have been much easier if we hadn't bothered to try and make our analytical system meaningful; in the analysis of informal discourse, it seems that one obtains reliability and inclusiveness at the expense of going against what seems intuitively to be meaningful.) And in any case, we realised that the categories we had arrived at so far were based on a small and homogeneous sample of children, working in a very narrow range of situations. It seemed preposterous to use this 'category system' as a measuring device in the testing of other variables; on the contrary, we felt that a good deal more substantive work would need to be done to check the applicability and validity of the analytical categories we had arrived at so far.

A further problem was that transcription and analysis of the groups' talk was taking much longer, and proving more difficult than anticipated. An adequate statistical design would have necessitated larger numbers of children than we could hope to transcribe and analyse in the time remaining to us.

At this point, we should perhaps have sat down to reconsider our best strategy in the light of these problems. However, the initial proposal to SSRC had promised to look at the effects of task and contextual conditions on the groups' communication; and although it was obvious that we could not do this in any rigorous way for the reasons given above, we felt an obligation at least to try to investigate these features, albeit in a much more limited fashion than first hoped. We therefore planned a quasi-experimental procedure for our second wave of data collection.

Selection of children: second phase of data collection

We worked with 24 children, 12 boys and 12 girls, who worked in 8 single-sex groups with 3 people in each group. We worked only at School X this time, largely because there were teachers there who were willing to make time to work with us. Again, we wanted to exclude children who were either exceptionally bright or of exceptionally low ability. This time, instead of relying on teachers' ratings, we had the A.H.4 administered to three classes in the third year, and selected for our sample children scoring in the middle band only. (The testing was carried out for us by a temporarily employed Research Assistant. We did not want the children to encounter either of us in the role of test administrator, since we felt that this could radically affect the quality of their participation in the groups' discussions later.)

The tasks

These eight groups of children were recorded working on two different tasks, which we expected to be different in the approach they elicited. Task A was what we called a 'Real Life' task, drawn from the area of social sciences, but potentially related to the children's own experiences and their knowledge of the everyday world. In brief, the children were asked to discuss what might be the causes of gang violence. The task card gave very little direction to the children, merely presented the question and asked them to discuss it.

Task B came from the physical sciences. The children had already been given a demonstration in class of the effects of differential air pressure on a corked bottle in a bell jar. They were asked to extrapolate from this to two comparable cases, a spaceship with a hole in it, and a man in space without a spacesuit. This was a far more 'tight' task, in that it directed the children to work through a series of questions in a certain order. (Both of these tasks are given in the Appendix.)

Contextual conditions

The children worked on these two tasks in two contextual conditions.
Under the 'Non-Assess' condition, they were told that their teacher
would neither be allowed to listen to the tape nor see a transcription of their talk. Under the 'Assess' condition they were
told that the teacher would listen to the tape of their talk to see
how they had done, and also that this group discussion was meant to
be a preparation for written work they would have to do on this same
topic next day; they were told that this written work would be collected in and marked by their teacher. In fact none of the work was
to be assessed by the teacher, nor were they really asked to do
written work.

Task, situation and procedure

The procedure for this set of recordings had to be different from
our usual practice. In the first place, all the groups had to be
recorded on the same day, to minimise disruption to the three
classes involved. This meant that we had to follow something of a
production line procedure, in order to fit them all in. Children
arrived to be recorded at the time specified, and left, to be
followed by other children. We introduced the situation with a
small amount of friendly chat, and read out the task card as usual.
Like our first groups, these children were also shown how to use the
tape recorder, and told to turn it off when they felt they had
finished. At a superficial inspection, the task situation for these
children might seem to be not too dissimilar from our first set of
recordings. But when we thought about it afterwards, we realised
that there were several important differences, and that it was these
accidental features, rather than what we had meant to be 'independent variables' which affected the quality of their talk.
   First, we want to summarise what these differences were, before
going on to discuss the significance of their effect more fully.

   (a)   In the first phase of recordings, we progressively became
         acquainted with the children, developing an amicable and re-
         laxed relationship with them. In the second phase, the
         first and only contact we had with these children was when
         they came to be recorded.
   (b)   The first phase children came from the same class and
         therefore knew each other. As far as possible they worked
         in groups approximating to their friendship patterns. The
         second phase children were selected from three different
         classes. (This was necessary in order to get enough
         children of the right sex in the middle range of ability.)
         As this was a big school, with a large third year, this en-
         tailed children working together who did not know one an-
         other well.
   (c)   In the second phase, because we were using children from
         different classes, we had to get the recording done in one
         day, or at the most a day and a half, to minimise dis-
         ruption to teachers. This meant we had to have a fast and

efficient turn-around of groups. So we did not have time
to play back their tape to them, to encourage questions
about what we were doing and so on, and certainly were not
able to establish any kind of personal relationship with
the children. We could not give them much time to overcome
their unease; we could not do preliminary recording and
playback to accustom them to the sound of their own voices.

(d)   Children in the first phase had a relaxed time schedule:
they could talk for as long as they wanted. We had to stop
the second lot of children after fifteen minutes even if
they had not quite finished.

(e)   The first phase children had a different time perspective:
they knew we would be visiting and recording again. The
second phase children knew it was a one-off affair, where
our purposes must have seemed very strange to them, and they
were part of a busy atmosphere of to-ing and fro-ing. There
were too many other children involved, and the turn-around
was too rapid, for them to feel that we had a personal
interest in them as individuals.

The 'experimental' analysis

In addition to the qualitative analysis which will be described in
Chapter 2 we attempted a quantitative analysis of the talk produced
in our quasi-experimental study. We looked at the following parameters:

(a)   the effects of contextual condition ('Assess' and 'Non-
Assess') on the 'correctness' of groups' answers ('correctness' being defined as acceptability to their teacher);

(b)   how many 'new' topics were generated under the two conditions ('new' topics being defined as those related to the
task but not given on the task card);

(c)   the effects of the contextual conditions on the amount of
time they spent actually trying to solve the problem as opposed to time spent repeating and checking their solution
so as to commit it to memory;

(d)   the effects of contextual conditions on the number of times
they tried to answer each question.

We abandoned the quantitative analysis because it became apparent:

(a)   that there were only minimal differences between groups'
performances on the 'Spaceman' task under 'Assess' and 'Non-
Assess' conditions;

(b)   that such differences as there were, surprisingly, related
to sex more than to anything else, i.e. girls got fewer
'right' answers, in more attempts than boys, and generated
fewer 'new' task related topics;

(c)   that even these overall sex differences were largely derived
from the performance of one particular group of girls, who
panicked;

(d)   that the quality of the talk and of the solutions offered
      by these groups was poorer than that obtained in our first
      phase of recordings;
(e)   that any attempt at statistical analysis would have ne-
      cessitated making some rather unreasonable assumptions about
      aspects of the measurement process involved.

We were most disappointed, not by being unable to produce a neat
set of significant differences, but by the quality of the children's
talk in this second phase of recording. We have already outlined
(Section 2) the differences between the two phases of recordings in
the way the situation was presented to the children. We now want to
look at the consequences of these differences.
    It is a commonplace of psychological testing and experimentation
(2) that subjects generate their own set of interpretations and
postulated reasons for the procedures they take part in, despite the
official account given to them by the investigator. In much the
same way, we suspect that the children in our second phase of
recordings interpreted what we were doing as being a 'test', regardless of the account we gave to them. This is borne out by the
questions of children who were theoretically working under the 'Non-
Assess' condition: some asked why they were being tested, and re-
mained unconvinced by the investigator's assurances that they were
not being tested at all. This implies that all the children were
working under a subjectively generated 'Assess' condition, a postu-
lation which would account both for the strained quality of the
talk, and the lack of differences between 'Assess' and 'Non-Assess'
groups.
    This subjective context can be accounted for in the following
ways:

(a)   the investigators were strangers;
(b)   the possibility that the children associated them with the
      IQ test of some weeks before;
(c)   the children's expectations of the evaluative practices
      normal in schools;
(d)   their interpretations of the particular lesson in which
      their teacher presented the subject-matter in question.

These together would be capable of persuading the children to interpret the context in ways quite contrary to our intentions.
    We describe this in some detail since other investigators may
similarly be tempted to record discussion under apparently 'controlled' conditions, and to ignore the effects of children's interpretations of context upon their communicative behaviour. There
do not seem to be short cuts to the understanding of conversation.
Data collected in one context should not be generalised to others
without the greatest care.

3 WHY WITHDRAW THE CHILDREN FROM THE CLASSROOM?

It could be argued that in withdrawing our children from the
classroom in order to record them we were creating an artificial and

special situation. Why didn't we record instead small group work
that took place in the classroom, as part of the normal day's work?

One very important reason for this choice is purely technical:
prior experience indicated that recordings made in a room where
thirty or so children were working would have been largely un-tran-
scribable, because of the volume and variety of background noise.
The only way to overcome this problem would be to use neck-micro-
phones, but the cost of these, and a mixer, would have been far
beyond the budget of our project. Obviously what one would gain
from recording group work in class would be a set of data far closer
to what ordinarily goes on in schools than the data which we have
collected.

A further, and equally important, consideration was the realisation that very few teachers use any substantial amount of small
group work, even those who express commitment and interest in it.
(We have already mentioned the discrepancies between the children's
and the teachers' perceptions of the amount of group work that they
did.) If we had only recorded group work that was 'naturally' occurring, we would have waited a long time to record a very small
number of group discussions. So, we decided to trade 'naturalness'
in exchange for an audible volume of children's talk. We have no
reason to regret this decision; on the contrary, we feel that it
was partly the very 'specialness' of the situation which called
forth such good efforts from the children. The talk produced by the
children was largely of a very high standard, in that they succeeded
in collaboratively coping with rather taxing cognitive and social
demands. Certainly their teachers were impressed at the quality of
their talk, and often felt that nothing like this was said in class.
So there seem to be very good reasons for putting children in a
situation which elicits their optimum performance; otherwise one
may never find out what they are capable of. Because we have chosen
to record in a context unlike a typical lesson, it will not be appropriate to apply what we say about children's uses of language to
classroom talk in general without making qualifications about the
social context offered by the classroom in question.

4   TRANSCRIPTION OF TAPES

Even though we were using a stereo tape recorder and two microphones, we still found transcription of the tapes a very difficult
and time-consuming task. Our basic procedure was for the project's
secretary to go through the tapes first, and produce a rough draft.
Then we would go through this draft over and over again, filling in
gaps, and making corrections. The major difficulties lay in (a)
transcribing utterances that were spoken simultaneously with other
utterances (b) attributing utterances to speakers (the children's
voices often sounded very alike on tape) and (c) catching utterances
that were spoken relatively softly, or with the speaker's head
turned away from the microphone.

It is not really possible to estimate how many hours of transcription there were for each hour of tape, since this varied according to particular features of different groups. We do feel that
transcription took a great deal more time than was allowed for in

the project's original outline, and similar projects in the future, which also intended to work on accurate texts, would need to take account of this. One rough figure we have seen is the suggestion that one should allow about ten hours of transcription time for each hour of tape. When we include the time our secretary spent on transcribing, as well as our own, and the time spent re-typing increasingly accurate texts, this seems an underestimate by perhaps 50 per cent.

Of course, we did not only focus on utterances in our transcriptions; equally interesting were the gaps between. Indeed, the very term 'utterance' is in one sense the embodiment of a set of theoretical constructs about talking which imply that utterances are discrete entities with beginnings and endings. The typical way of presenting utterances on paper is to lay them out like the script of a play, speakers' names to the left, and speeches to the right. Everyday conversation is a good deal less tidy than this, however, and it is not easy to decide where one utterance ends and another begins. We found ourselves relying on the lengths of pauses to help decide this, and we show pauses in our scripts via a somewhat specialised use of commas, full stops and dotted lines. Short pauses (as for intake of breath) are shown by a comma; pauses of longer duration which were still too short to measure in terms of the tape recorder's revolution counter system are indicated by three dots. Pauses of longer duration still are given in our transcripts in terms of the recorder's counter numbers.

5 QUALITATIVE RATHER THAN QUANTITATIVE ANALYSIS

At the beginning of this chapter we said that our original intentions were to set up analytical systems which identified functional characteristics of utterances, and then to relate these to verbal forms which 'realised' these functions. For example, we thought that the tentative-dogmatic dimension would be related to the distribution of forms such as modal auxiliaries (3) and of such expressions as 'You could say that...' which often have a similar modal function. Similarly, we thought that the extent to which the children were attending to and utilising one another's viewpoints would show itself in the frequency of forms linking one utterance to another in sequential discourse.

Our attempts to identify the linguistic forms which carried out these functions had to be abandoned, since in the course of them we concluded that the attempts themselves were out of place. In effect, it seemed that a direct relationship between form and meaning could not reasonably be assumed. We were forced to this conclusion because, first, there appeared to be a lack of match between the functional categories which we set up and the incidence of the forms postulated to carry out these functions, and second, in some cases forms were clearly ambiguous, and open to more than one functional interpretation. A phrase such as 'Well, it all depends...' may mark a genuine acknowledgment of the validity of another's point of view, or may be no more than a tactful gesture; it is often impossible to determine from the materials which of these interpretations is more valid. Moreover, it appeared that in

our materials the tentativeness/dogmatism function was carried out
more by intonation than by the modal forms which we had looked for.
Considerations such as these caused us to doubt whether forms should
ever be assigned to unique functions, and to abandon attempts to
classify and quantify them. Our concern in the study was with communication and learning, so that this directed us towards meanings
rather than towards forms. Furthermore, if forms alone do not determine meaning, it must be determined also by the bodies of
knowledge brought to the understanding of those forms.

We are conscious that this view - which we have been compelled to
take up by our data, against the current of our initial expectations - runs contrary to the assumptions of those researchers who
have quantified the distribution of language forms and used this
data as evidence of cognitive structures. We do not believe that
linguistic forms and meanings are related in a way which would
justify this.

For example, M.A.K.Halliday, whose work has been specially valuable because of its orientation to the social contexts of speech,
nevertheless assumes that a semantic system would in theory be
parallel to the system of linguistic forms through which it was (in
his term)'realised'. He argues that 'the semantic options are re-
latable to recognizable features in the grammar, even though the relationship will often be rather a complex one'.(4) Thus in
Halliday's view it is theoretically possible to proceed from (a) a
sociological analysis of 'situation types', through (b) an analysis
of 'meaning potential' in each situation and (c) an analysis of the
'functional components' of the meaning potential, to (d) an analysis
of grammatical structures.(5)

We believe that in positing this ideal relationship between
meaning potential and its formal exponents Halliday is ignoring the
many diverse systems of meaning available to members of a speech
community, and available to a lesser extent to each of them as
options. By assuming a determinate relationship between grammatical
systems and bodies of knowledge Halliday leaves out of account the
negotiations between alternative bodies of knowledge which we
believe we observe in our materials. Our groups were negotiating
not only what knowledge of subject-matter should be treated as relevant to the task in hand, but were also negotiating the social relationships which were to obtain between themselves. We call these
two bodies of knowledge 'Content Frames' and 'Interaction Frames',
and in Chapter 4 discuss how they are negotiated.

COLLABORATION AND TEXTUAL COHESION

One of our initial interests was the likely effects upon children's
understanding of having to attend to another person's different
viewpoint, and of having to make their own viewpoints explicit to
someone who did not share them. This led us on the one hand towards
'reflexivity', and on the other towards signs that group members
were attending to one anothers' points of view and utilising them in
their own thinking.

We thought that, if a speaker is responding in detail to what has
just been said by others, this might well be represented by re-

lationships between the verbal structures of succeeding utterances.
We spent some time in attempting to analyse sequences of utterances
using various markers of textual cohesion. Although these clearly
had some importance in the sequence of thought, the relationship between semantic content seemed at least as important. Moreover,
since in some well-established groups the communication, though
successful, was highly eliptical, our identification of cohesion
features seemed irrelevant to the question of collaborative thought.
After spending considerable time on this approach we eventually
abandoned it: we doubt whether there is a consistent relationship
between the distribution of cohesion features and the extent to
which group members are trying to assimilate and use one another's
viewpoints.
    Amongst the cohesion features considered were the following:

1   Anaphora (6)
2   Repetitions of content words
3   Repetitions of content words with morphological changes
4   Repetitions of syntactic structures
5   Repetitions of syntactic structures with transformations
6   Syntactic and other indicators of logical relationships
    between utterances

From a formal linguist's point of view there do seem to be matters
of interest in this line of thought, though they were not relevant
to our task. Our interest was not to find out how all dialogue is
structured, but to recognise structures in dialogue which contribute
to learning.

7   DIFFICULTIES IN CATEGORISING DATA OF THIS KIND

The problems which we encountered in attempting to set up a category
system will be very familiar to anyone who has attempted to work on
talk produced in an informal situation, for talk produced in such a
context lacks the manifestations of structure common in other situations. The analysis of discourse in education has focussed more on
situations where talk is relatively well-structured according to a
set of social conventions, such as teacher-pupil talk in the
classroom.(7) In this situation the context of the interaction
itself induces a set of relatively formalised norms for the
structure of the discourse, whereas the rules for the shaping of
interaction in our groups were more open to negotiation. We do not
mean that there were no constraints upon them: obviously, they were
at school rather than at home, or a discoteque, and they knew they
were being recorded. They had also been asked to do something which
presumably approximated more closely to their definition of 'school-
work' than to anything else like 'watching television', or
'chatting-up', but it is important to note that these constraints
were not formalised or ritualised as they are in the contexts on
which classroom analysis has usually focussed. In some ways, despite the presence of the tape-recorder, we feel that the talk we
obtained from the children is closer to conversations where people
talk for their own purposes, than it is to classroom talk, where the

purposes of the teacher provide the dominant framework. Certainly,
there is a fluid, dynamic quality to the talk that the children
produced. And although this structural complexity makes the talk
delightful to listen to, these same fluid and dynamic features also
make it inappropriate to pin the talk down into a category system.

There are two special difficulties which are worth elaborating,
and which represent well the paradoxical nature of free-flowing
talk. These are that on the one hand, a very great deal may go on
in just one utterance: the observer may feel that several equally
important things are happening at the same time. He cannot put
utterances into categories on a one-to-one basis, because some
utterances seem to belong in several categories. On the other hand,
it also seems that meanings for what is going on in the conversation are constructed not from any one utterance on its own, but
from cycles of utterances, perhaps over quite lengthy sections of
the interaction. Now these cycles are not readily isolable: they
adhere to the interaction between utterances, and the speaker-
hearer's intentions for, and interpretation of, these utterances.
When we analyse talk, what we are trying to do is to feel our way
into the meanings the participants made for the interaction as it
happened. But the meanings which the participants made were not
stable. They were fluid and changing, built up out of the existing
knowledge and expectations which they brought to the situation,
along with their own implicit summary of what went on in the conversation, and their reaction to that summary. Meanings change in
response to on-going events in the conversation, which lead to a
reinterpretation of what has gone on so far. (This view of the
construction of meaning through talk is expanded in Chapter 4.)

All of these features lead to grave problems for anyone who
wishes to categorise talk. For it often seems that the features
which are most visible, most readily isolable, are those which are
least important: whilst those features which the observer focusses
on as being most significant are precisely those which are hardest
to categorise in a reliable way.

It was clear to us that in these conversations much more was
happening than as observers we could hope to be aware of, much less
describe. Moreover, our concentration on the language at the
expense of the paralinguistic channels of communication again
narrowed our range of reference. Our approach has been to separate
out from the very complex meanings negotiated in the discussions
some of the more visible phenomena in order to make sense of these.
This has necessitated the assumption that the meanings we have assigned to these more visible phenomena are in some way representative of other meanings out of our reach; this assumption, though
clearly open to dispute, seems to be forced on anyone who investi-
gates this kind of data. Under these circumstances any attempt to
create rigorous and exclusive category systems would have been out
of place and misleading.

Observers construct meanings via a process very similar to that
carried out by the original participants: they too must use their
intuitions to try to interpret what the talk means. Because we had
made sound recordings only, our data was limited in that the non-
verbal features of the communication were lost to us. Since the
categorisations we made were largely intuitive, they were open to

error, but no more open to error than categorisations which purport
to be objective. This is a difficulty which is faced by anyone
working on discourse. One solution to this problem that has been
used by some workers (8) is to play back the recording of the interaction to the original participants, and check out with them what
they intended their utterances to mean and how they interpreted
other speakers. We had neither the time nor the resources to do
this. But this strategy does not give a final solution, because
even for the participants in a conversation, meaning is not static.
Reflecting upon a conversation which is past, where one can stop the
tape to check back on unclear bits, is not the same as taking part
in a conversation. Perhaps the most important difference is that
once the conversation is over, one knows where it went to, one knows
the sequence of speech events which followed other events; whereas
during the on-going flux of conversation, what will follow the
speech event that is happening now is unknown. Once a conversation
is 'past' rather than 'now', although one can alter one's own interpretation of what happened, one cannot unsay what was said;
whereas the participant in an on-going conversation is constantly
choosing what to say and what to leave unsaid, that is, he has a set
of options which are closed off to the listener after-the-event.
The fact that one does not have these options for action, only
options for retrospective interpretation, makes listening to a
conversation that is past very different from taking part in one;
so that for the participants in a conversation, their retrospective
account of 'what happened' will be different from their on-going
account of 'what is happening'.
    Given that the interpretation of conversational meanings by an
observer is problematic, there are ways in which he can attempt to
limit the introduction of bias. Coombs (9) has argued that 'all
facts are inferences' but this does not mean that an observer cannot
explain the scope of the inferences which he makes. Our strategy
was to attempt to start from the data (acknowledging that even to
speak of the existence of something one calls 'data' is in effect a
theoretical formulation), and to work from the data towards a category system. We spent a lot of time, going over transcripts together, listening repeatedly to the tapes; from this would come a
tentative notion about a way of categorising, which we would use to
apply to the transcripts to see if it 'fitted'. Often, it did not,
and we would have to start again. So the categories that we have
finally arrived at are 'grounded' (10) in the data, in that they
have developed out of a series of successive approximations, rather
than being a pre-existing grid which we have imposed on the data
from above.
    Our gravest doubt about our categories is whether they do, in
fact, conserve those features of the children's talk which we see
as theoretically important. We are interested in learning, in cognition, in the construction by the children of some of their own
knowledge. We recorded children talking together in the hope that
we could distinguish knowledge in the process of being made during
their co-operative effort. The difficulty is to decide how crucial
is the presence of any particular linguistic and interactional
features. Those we find striking may merely represent the habitual
style of these particular children. Perhaps other children would

create equally valid and complex solutions to the same problems
without using any of the same verbal strategies. This is a doubt
we have to live with: our analysis is based upon what these
children did.

8   THE DESCRIPTIVE SYSTEM USED

We began by following Halliday and the linguists of the Prague
school (11) in distinguishing three functional components of speech
acts: Ideational, Interpersonal and Textual. For reasons discussed
above, we have not followed Halliday in relating these functions to
specifiable language forms which are their exponents. It has proved
valuable to retain the distinction between social (interactive) and
cognitive aspects of speech events. We have however subdivided
these into two levels which provide four functional components
instead of Halliday's three.

	Interaction	Cognition
Level One:	(i) Discourse Moves	(ii) Logical Process
Level Two:	(iii) Social Skills	(iv) Cognitive Strategies

These will now be discussed in turn. (Table 2 summarises the social
and cognitive functions of conversation; they are illustrated and
discussed in Chapter 2.)

(i)   Discourse Moves

These are related to Halliday's 'textual' function. They include
those characteristics which any discourse must have in order to be
coherent and sequential: without such sequential relationships
there would not be a conversation but only a list of sentences. We
have sketched out moves such as Initiating, which might be followed
by Responding, Extending, or Eliciting. Such a system could be made
exhaustive, but we have chosen not to pursue this line of thought.
This is partly because it does not seem central to understanding the
relationship between verbalisation and learning; and partly because
the work of Sinclair and his associates is currently focussed on the
development of a scheme at this level of analysis. (12)

(ii)   Logical Process

It is this component which we have added to Halliday's three. The
coherence indicated in discourse analysis is typified by what in
everyday language would be called the relationship between a
question and an answer. Even when it is acknowledged that much of
the discourse function is probably carried by intonation, there is
still a considerable element of cohesion in dialogue which is not
attributable to those features which Halliday calls 'textual'. This
cohesion arises as much from common content as from the movement of
initiative in the discourse. We first attempted to describe this -

TABLE 2 Social and cognitive functions of conversation

LEVEL ONE

(i) Discourse Moves

(a) Initiating	(b) Extending	(c) Eliciting	(d) Responding
	Qualifying	- Continue Expand Bring in Support Information	Accepting
	Contradict- ing		

(ii) Logical Process

    (a) Proposes a cause

    (b) Proposes a result

    (c) Expands loosely (e.g. descriptive details)

    (d) Applies a principle to a case

    (e) Categorises

    (f) States conditions under which statement is valid or invalid

    (g) Advances evidence

    (h) Negates

    (i) Evaluates

    (j) Puts alternative view

    (k) Suggests a method

    (l) Restates in different terms

LEVEL TWO

(iii) Social Skills

(a) Progress through task	Given questions Shifting topic Ending a discussion Managing manipulator tasks
(b) Competition and conflict	Competition for the floor Contradiction Joking Compelling participation
(c) Supportive behaviour	Explicit agreement Naming Reference back Explicit approval of others Expression of shared feeling

(iv) Cognitive Strategies

1	Constructing the question	'Closed' tasks Open tasks
2	Raising new questions	
3	Setting up hypotheses	Beyond the given Explicit hypotheses
4	Using evidence	Anecdote Hypothetical cases Using every-day knowledge Challenging generalities
5	Expressing feelings and recreating experience	Expressing ethical judgments Shared recreation of literary experience

(v) Reflexivity

(a)	Monitoring own speech and thought	own contributions provisional
(b)	Interrelating alternative viewpoints	validity to others more than one possibility finding overarching principles
(c)	Evaluating own and others' performance	
(d)	Awareness of strategies	audience for recording summarising moving to new topic

---

which we call the 'logical process' - by making a content analysis
of a topic and then identifying for each utterance both its content
category and its logical relationship to a previous utterance. By
showing which member of the group contributed each utterance it
would be possible to represent schematically the pattern of thought-
development in a discussion. This form of analysis did not prove
useful, because the logical relationships in our materials are more
often left implicit than given verbal form, so that the logical
antecedents of utterances are frequently ambiguous or diffuse.
This indeterminacy, we concluded, was functional in such conversations, and should not be obscured by an idealising logical analysis. Nevertheless, we present in Table 2 our list of logical
processes for completeness, since they appear to parallel in the
Cognitive domain the discourse moves in the Interaction domain.

(iii) Social Skills

Our purpose in this study has been to identify speech events related
to the shaping of understanding. The analytical categories for
discourse and logical sequence seemed from the first unsatisfactory
for this purpose because, while they described unquestionable
characteristics of conversation, these characteristics did not seem
closely related to the learning upon which our study was focussed.
It was as if discourse analysis and logical analysis were directed
towards small scale phenomena, whereas the choices significant for
learning were being made on a larger scale. Moreover, whereas
utterances lacking first-level phenomena would not constitute discourse, it was perfectly possible to envisage discussion which
lacked those ways of organising social relationships or organising
thought which we were interested in. That is, we wanted to identify
aspects of talk which contributed to learning, even if these occurred only irregularly.

   For this reason we have adopted a different strategy for our
second-level components, Social Skills and Cognitive Strategies.
We have not attempted to set up two exhaustive category systems,
with discrete categories objectively defined. Rather we have chosen
to describe informally in Chapter 2 what thirteen-year-old boys and
girls are able to achieve in conversation when set group learning
tasks under the conditions described above.

   Amongst the requirements for coherent and productive group
problem-solving are the ability to control the group's progress
through the task, the management of competition and conflict, and
the giving of mutual support. We have observed examples of these
in our materials, and under the heading of Social Skills have set
out to identify these abilities and to illustrate them. It will be
clear that these exist on a different level of generality from the
discourse moves: a social skill such as 'Ending a discussion' might
be made up of several discourse moves. On the other hand, 'Joking',
though perhaps 'realised' by no more than a phrase, appears to
operate at a similar level of generality to 'Ending a discussion'.
We are here pointing to voluntary social strategies, though by
'voluntary' we do not necessarily imply a high level of reflective
self-awareness.

(iv) Cognitive Strategies

Similarly, the component called Cognitive Strategies constitutes a
group of rather general voluntary thought-processes carried out more
or less explicitly in words. These are separated from Social Skills
solely for purposes of analysis: in reality, Cognitive Strategies
are carried out by means of Social Skills, and Social Skills are
identified by their contribution to Cognitive Strategies. Thus it
may be possible to identify a particular utterance as an instance
both of a Social Skill and of a Cognitive Strategy. (At the same
time parts of it could probably be identified as a set of Discourse
Moves and as falling into Logical Process categories.)

   The Cognitive Strategies selected include constructing a meaning
for a set question, inventing a problem where none was set, setting

up hypotheses, using evidence, and recreating experience. These were chosen because we had observed examples of them in the materials, and judged that such strategies might have general importance in the carrying out of school learning tasks. Cognitive Strategies at this level are likely to be more significant for school learning than are the single-move logical links of which they are made and which we allocate to the component called Logical Process.

We have also isolated under the heading of 'Reflexivity' certain other occasions when the pupils showed a higher degree of self-awareness either in the Social Skills they were using or in the Cognitive Strategies which they adopted. These constitute a partly arbitrary selection from the Social and Cognitive strategies; they occurred less frequently than most of the other strategies of each kind. We chose thus to emphasise the conscious, reflective element in these strategies mainly because of our initial interest in noticing when group discussion moved towards the reflexive thought patterns characteristic of Piaget's 'formal operations'. In fact, we have no reason to suggest any direct relationship between these reflexive strategies and formal operations, nor can we assert with any confidence that the reflexive moves played a central part in the group's thinking when they were used. Some of our examples are, however, suggestive, and might give directions for further investigation.

The analysis of Cognitive Strategies and of Reflexivity can be said to take the place of the analysis into 'cognitive levels' which was originally proposed. It proved impossible to apply Peel's categories (13) to the analysis of dialogue, first because the structures of meaning expressed were for the most part not explicit enough to be assigned confidently to a level; and second, because it became clear that when group members were using the same words they often differed widely in the use they were able to put them to. That s, it is not possible to read off a hierarchy of thought from a verbal structure.

Having turned our attention away from forms of language as indicators of learning, we turned towards the children's application of knowledge to the tasks put before them. Although children have at their disposal complex bodies of implicit knowledge about the world, teachers frequently control classroom knowledge in such a way that pupils appear ignorant. We were interested to see how children utilised this knowledge in a context in which, although the overall relevances lay in the teacher's control (through the setting of the task), the pupils controlled both their step by step strategies and their social relationships.

MAKING SENSE TOGETHER

1 COLLABORATION IN THE GROUPS

Our first task is to show that thirteen-year-olds can indeed work
together, and in discussing a topic with one another can collaborate
in clarifying their own and one another's understanding of it.
Underlying this discussion of episodes from their talk will be the
assumption that by talking one may clarify one's own understanding,
as well as communicating with others.

Throughout this chapter we offer interpretive accounts of the
extracts, either as a parallel commentary or below the extract.
We regard these as no more than hypothetical reconstructions, put
forward as a basis for discussion. (In Chapter 4 we discuss the
nature and limitations of observers' accounts of conversation.)
When the commentary is set out beside the text we suggest that the
reader should first read the text alone, and then reread it with
our commentary.

We begin by looking at how one of our groups (Group 4) starts to
discuss the topic set to them. They had been asked to discuss how
a National Park in the Lake District might set out to reconcile
demands for providing facilities for outdoor pursuits and tourism
with the need to preserve the natural landscape and protect farming.
(See the Appendix for the text of this and the other tasks set.)

| 1 Alan: | Do you think this is a good idea for big National Parks? | Initiates discussion by raising an issue not set on the task card. |
| | I think it is a, an excellent idea because, erm, people like us have the erm, countryside around us, but other people in the, erm, centre of Leeds are less fortunate and do not have erm, centre – countryside that they can go out into within easy reach. | Answers his own questions and sets up a context for the ensuing discussions of the set questions. (1) (N.B. The school attended by these children is amidst fields on the outskirts of the city.) |

2 Bill:	Yeah	Provides encouragement.
3 Alan:	Without being polluted and erm, chimney stacks all over the place.	Makes the antithesis more explicit.
4 Pauline:	This is all right as long as there in't gonna be too many buildings around the place, 'cos it's gonna spoil it completely I think. It's all right for a few like cafés or, er, camping sites, a few camping sites. That's all right but nothing else.	Qualifies Alan's contributions, thus turning the discussion towards the set questions. She reinforces part of what Alan said, but suggests that limits need to be drawn.
5 Alan:	I think this is one of the best ideas of the erm, National Parks because they erm do not, don't allow buildings to be built without permissions and planning special, you know, so it blends with the countryside and not stuck out like a sore thumb.	Accepts the qualification which leads to his extending the concept of National Parks to include the regulation of building.
6 Jeanette:	Yeah, but it just depends on what the ground's like dun't it?	Qualifies that part of Alan's statement that refers to blending with the countryside.

We put this passage forward to illustrate how a group can under some circumstances collaborate from the start on the coherent and rational construction of understanding. In this case the ideas are ones likely to be readily available from everyday life, though the topic had previously been discussed in a lesson. There is no sense of the regurgitation of inert knowledge, however, or of the retracing of a familiar path; the girls and boys are rearranging their knowledge as they talk, and trying out new combinations and implications.

The topic in our next example is, in contrast, scientific. Another group (Group 1) has been given these definitions: 'We use the idea of WORK as a measure of how much ENERGY changes from one form to another. WORK is done when a force moves.' The pupils were required to apply these definitions to three given examples, and then to think of other examples of energy changes, in order to answer the question, 'Is work always done when energy changes form?' In this case too the group had had preliminary discussion of the topic in class. In answering the question, however, they had to utilise both ideas from everyday life and the given definitions of work and energy. The following exchange occurred when, after some minutes of discussion the group had dealt with the three given examples.

48 Marianne:	Is, is there any things that we don't use energy in?	Marianne seeks an example to test an earlier assertion by Barbara.
49 David:	Yeah	
50 Marianne:	What?	
51 David:	Erm, one of these, one of these pylons, holding up a roof, they aren't using energy.	Puts forward a relevant example.
52 Jonathan:	It's constant energy, 'cos if that wasn't there the roof'd fall.	Jonathan does not use the given test for the change of energy from one form to another, but appears to be using a concept equivalent to 'potential energy'.
53 David:	No, it in't moving is it? So it can't be using any energy.	David, using the definition of 'work' challenges Jonathan's assertion.
54 Jonathan:	Well it had to use energy in the first place to be put up though.	Changes his statement to a form which acknowledges the validity of the test.
55 Marianne:	Well it's using work (1)	Not (apparently) using the given definition of 'work'.
56 David:	Oh to be put up yeah, but when it's there now, it just holds the roof up. It in't moving; it doesn't have energy.	David summarises, relating to one another the two versions of energy previously put forward; he lacks a term such as 'potential energy' for labelling one of them.
57 Jonathan:	There's a force, as well though	Checking their agreement on the distinction between 'force' and 'energy'.
58 David:	I know there'll be loads of force but there won't be any energy	As above.
59 Jonathan:	Uhm, no moving energy	Jonathan is able to summarise because he has now fully assimilated the

		definition of energy via work.
60 David:	There won't be any energy doing even...	Incomplete
61 Jonathan:	There's no energy trans-ferred from one to't other is there?	Now begins to move on to a further concept, ac-cepting what has gone before.

What we have here is a serious and fruitful discussion in which David, Jonathan and Marianne help one another to apply the given definitions to a new case. They make mistakes, but they address themselves to the task in a purposive and rational manner. In understanding that this is so we have often to detach our awareness of the style of speech from the content. Although the conversations are often informal in tone and - in comparison with a written textbook - pursue an indirect path, this should not prevent us from appreciating that a necessary kind of learning is going on.

The two examples so far quoted show groups working so successful-ly that they hardly encourage the reader to ask: What do children have to be able to do in order to construct knowledge jointly in this way? How do they set about contributing to the discussion, and how do they receive what others say? How do they invite contri-butions from others, and how do they interrelate or reconcile different viewpoints? We shall now examine in more detail the moves which make up the complex discussions which we have been consider-ing. In these two short examples we found these moves being made:

initiating discussion of a new issue	Group 4 No. 1
qualifying another preson's contribution	4
implicitly accepting a qualification	5
extending a previous contribution	6
asking for an illustration to test a generali-sation	Group 1 No.48
providing an example	51
using evidence to challenge an assertion	53
reformulating one's own previous assertion	54

This list ignores social functions such as encouragement - which will be discussed later - and also those more indefinable moves which cannot be summed up in a phrase. (Examples of these more com-plex moves can be found in Group 1's utterances, Nos 56 and 59, in which the two boys summarise the distinction so far arrived at in the discussion.) Elsewhere in our materials we have noted pupils:

    obtaining information from others
    completing unfinished utterances
    encouraging others to continue
    inviting others to contribute
    repeating with modifications
    supporting another's assertion with evidence

These can be ordered into four categories of collaborative moves:
initiating, eliciting, extending and qualifying. Our purpose here
is to hint at the many collaborative skills shown by thirteen-year-
olds, without which such group discussions could not take place.
Some of these skills belonging to the four categories will be illustrated in the rest of this section.

Initiating

We now illustrate how a new topic is initiated, using mainly
examples which follow a pause in the talk. Our first examples are
taken from discussions of the task which we call 'Vandalism', though
it was in fact concerned with the reasons why some adolescent boys
join in gang violence: the groups were given as their starting-
point part of a transcript of an interview with a former gang-leader
called Ron.
     In Group 1 (which the reader has already met in the science dis-
cussion) David begins with:
     I think the causes of vandalism er's boredom usually, in' it,
     can't find anything to do.
This is received with giggles and embarrassed silence so he tries
again:
     I think the area you live in er, could affect the way they behave
     because when there's other gangs around you, I think it er, you
     know make you want to fight too if you see em all, fighting and
     that, it looks like fun and so he'll just join in.
And this time the lead is taken up by the others.
     It seems important that one member of the group should take the
initiative and set up a frame of reference which will enable discussion to begin. Group 4 had little difficulty in finding leads:
even Jeanette's cryptic opening is quickly developed.
     13 Jeanette: I don't think there's any need for all this fight-
                    ing do you, but it can cause, cause harm.
     14 Bill: Oh, they just go looking for it.
     15 Jeanette: Yeah I know
     16 Bill: Well not just so ...
Jeanette's initiative has been taken up by Bill, and the other two
join in a few moments later.
     Later in the same discussion an initiative by Bill meets a chilly
fate:
     35 Bill: I don't think this last sentence in the interview
                    with Ron is very ... useful. I don't think it,
                    belongs there. I don't think it's any use at all
                    to the story.
But there the matter is left: the others are unable or unwilling to
take it up.
     Many initiating moves are introduced by 'I think' or 'I don't
think', which appears to indicate that as the speaker is raising a
new topic he regards its relevance and usefulness as open to the
others' judgment. Initiating moves do sometimes occur without the
'I think' introduction but they are then usually linked closely to
the task set to the group. For example, one boy in a discussion of
the 'Work and Energy' topic revived the talk after a pause by the
following:

Another energy change would be erm, heat from the sun erm, helping to produce flowers.
One might surmise that in this case the new issue followed so closely the pattern laid down in the task that he did not use 'I think'
because he did not regard its relevance as open to negotiation or
question.

Another case occurred when Group 4 were attempting a task which
we have not so far mentioned. They were given a draft of a letter
which purported to have been written by a boy, Steve, to his employer in order to break off temporary employment. The task was to
reconsider the abrasive tone of the letter in the light of the
possibility that Steve might later want further employment. After
talking for some minutes Group 4 fell silent, and Jeanette initiated
further discussion by quoting a sentence from the original letter.

26 Jeanette: 'You must think I'm crazy   Quotes from the letter a
               trying this one on me.'   sentence not yet discuss-
                                               ed, but does not set up
                                               any framework for ap-
                                               proaching it.

27 Pauline: I think that's all right.   Accepts the proffered
               (i.e. that sentence can   focus, and sets up a
               stand.)   framework of general ap-
                                               proval/disapproval for
                                               discussing the sentence.

Jeanette was not offering an opinion but merely - in a very open
way - putting forward a focus for attention. It is Pauline who is
committing herself to an approach and who therefore uses the 'I
think'.

Exchanges are often initiated by questions, many of these arising
directly from the task set. When Group 4 are working on the 'Work
and Energy' topic they move on to a new example thus:

25 Jeanette: Well what do you think   Invites a lead from one
               about (b) heat to movement   of the others by reading
               in a steam engine?   aloud one of the given
                                              questions.

27 Bill: I think that erm, well   Takes up the offered
               that's .... (etc.)   initiative.

In contrast with this, Group 3, having talked for a while about
questions set to them on Steinbeck's novel 'The Pearl', turn to a
question of their own: 'Do you think the book's any good so far?'
(Once again 'Do you think?' acknowledges the offering of the initiative.)

Eliciting

It is now time however to move from the initiating of discussions to
the more generally important matter of how groups sustain coherent

talk, and particularly how they invite one another to contribute.
Without some such mutual support it seems unlikely that a group
could sustain the uncertainties of a focussed discussion for any
length of time. We shall distinguish four kinds of eliciting moves:
(a) requests to someone to 'Continue' what they are saying; (b) requests to 'Expand' a previous remark; (c) requests for 'Support'
for the speaker's opinion; (d) requests for 'Information'.

Simple invitations to continue are rare in the discussions,
perhaps because they are potentially claims to a leadership role.
In Group 4's discussion of Steve's Letter, Alan begins:

28 Alan: Yea, I think you could start off like erm ...

and when he pauses, Bill's, 'Go on, go on', encourages him to continue.

More frequently invitations to continue are for explicit
purposes. By the time we reached the recording of the 'Steve's
Letter' discussion, Group 4 were giving one another a great deal of
support: this was not a matter of agreeing with one another, but of
attending closely to what was said and replying appropriately.

106 Pauline: I think he should just leave it: 'Dear Sir, You
               must think I'm crazy trying this one on me. Just
               light work. Do you think clearing up spit, ice
               cream and fag ends is easy work? You can keep
               it.'
107 Alan: Why, is that what you'd write?
108 Pauline: Yeah. Cos it's short and it's telling him, it's
               telling him right from the start.

Alan's question seems to be not so much an expression of surprise as
a request for Pauline to extend what she had said so as to confirm
his interpretation of her meaning; this is probably because she was
still using the abrasive tone of the original letter and this ran
counter to much of what had been previously said in the discussion.
The question 'Is that what you'd write?' contains implicitly not
only a request for confirmation but also for some justification: a
mere 'Yes' might have appeared stubborn or even aggressive, though
this would depend upon its intonation.

A slightly different request for expansion occurred when Group 5
attempted the 'Bird's Eggs' task, in which the pupils were required
to break the shell of an egg, to discuss what they observed, and to
answer questions which included, 'Do you think a bird's egg could be
fertilised inside the hen's body? What makes you think so?'

102 Donald: It's fertilised in't body, it must be. Course
              it's fertilised in't body.
103 Louise: ⌈What makes you think so?
104 Helen: ⌊It must be
105 David: 'Cos it wun't get back through
106 Helen: It can hardly get through't damn shell, can it?

Louise uses the question from the task card, 'What makes you think
so?' as if it were her own, and thereby draws a useful reply from
Helen at 106. Here the request to expand the previous assertion is
explicitly a request for a rational argument in support of it.
(This kind of eliciting move is the reciprocal of the 'Extending'
move which will be discussed below, though the latter frequently
occurs without having been explicitly elicited.)

The next form of eliciting move to be illustrated is the request for 'Support'. It is necessary to distinguish the general, almost habitual, appeals for confirmation from more particular ones. Throughout our materials we find frequent examples of statements followed by tag-questions of the 'isn't it?' 'hasn't he?' 'won't they?' kind. For example:

Yeah, well, the ground in't strong enough really, is it?
These often appear to be requests for reassurance that the channel is open and the audience attending, though when they occur at the end of an utterance they may signal 'Over to you' to the other participants. These general appeals, in conjunction with nods and eye-movements and sounds such as 'mm', undoubtedly play an important part in sustaining conversation. Here however we wish to place our emphasis upon appeals which, although often similar in form, operate as direct requests for explicit confirmation or denial of the statement. Group 1, discussing 'National Parks', show this example:

89 Jonathan:	We don't want any petrol stations, or not many, do we? (Sc. in National Parks)	Jonathan makes a firm statement, qualifies it uncertainly, and then asks for support
90 Barbara:	No, you have them in't villages as well	Barbara indicates agreement and supplies supporting evidence.

The last kind of eliciting moves differs from the others in being a request for 'Information', and is often quite explicitly focussed. Nevertheless, like the other kinds it tends to strengthen the group members' sense of controlling the knowledge which they are using since it ascribes validity to their own existing bodies of knowledge. As might be expected, such requests were particularly frequent in the discussions of 'The Pearl' since those pupils who had read further held information not available to the others. One example of this comes from Group 3:

    3 Robert: That doctor really cheats him because once he
                 hears about the pearl that Kino's found, he
                 changes his mind about coming to see Coyotito,
                 doesn't he?
    4 Margaret: He changes his mind
    5 Robin: Is it him who tries to pinch it when he's asleep?
Robin, who has not read as much of the novel as he should have done, is asking for help in linking the doctor with another incident in the book. The construction of a common interpretation plays an important part in adolescents' discussions of literature, and this is often initiated by similar requests for the elucidation of links between episodes.

In the absence of a teacher the group has no source of knowledge but themselves and whatever materials, apparatus or information that has been put in front of them. As a result their behaviour is very different from the typical behaviour of children in class: they consult the materials rather than watching for signals from a teacher; they test the interpretations which they have put forward by matching them with their existing sense of how things are. In a word, they treat one another as resources.

Extending

When a group has found a strategy which appears to be valuable in
pursuing the task, they often collaborate to carry it out, so that
one member takes an idea up from where another left it, and extends
it. Group 1, while discussing 'The Pearl', turn for a moment to the
verisimilitude of that part of the story in which Kino, the pearl-
diver, finds the enormous pearl.

49 Marianne:	It seems a bit unbelieva-ble, dun't it?	This is part of a fore-going discussion of veri-similitude.
50 David:	Yeah.	
51 Marianne:	Really, not realistic enough. He should have...	Interrupted.
52 David:	An er, an er, as big as his hand	(Perhaps) Offering part of the reason for scepti-cism.
53 Marianne:	Yeah, he should have had a bit more description, not about the pearl but about the actual diving, that he went down you know, and how, what clothes he wore and you know, what kind of things that he used.	Transmutes the judgment of verisimilitude into a demand for description, qualifying it to help the others understand her
54 Barbara:	What he felt when he found it...	Extends the idea towards Kino's subjective ex-perience.
55 Marianne:	Yeah	Confirms that Barbara has grasped her intention. (Or merely shows that she is attending?)
56 Barbara:	... the shell and that ...	Specifies the reference of 'it' in 54.
57 David:	Well when ...	Tries to enter
58 Marianne:	And how long he can hold ...	Suggests another detail for the description but is interrupted.
59 David:	Well when he came ...	Begins to make the contribution attempted at 57.
	... Well they described that, how long he held his breath.	Understands Marianne's incomplete remark and deals with it.

When, when he came up and when he, when he slipped a knife into it, it tightened up and he couldn't open it.	Returns to his original idea, which (implicitly) presents an example where Steinbeck had provided realistic detail of the kind required.
60 Marianne: Mm, that were good.	Makes explicit the appreciation implicit in David's contribution.

We have presented this sequence at some length to illustrate how skilfully a group may at best work together in taking up one another's ideas in order to extend them further, or to transmute them.

It is not at all unusual for two or three members of a group to construct a sentence jointly. A typical example comes from Group 1's discussion of 'National Parks':

```
20 David:     ⎡ I think bigger fines should be imposed for the
              ⎢ people who don't obey the country laws and thereby
              ⎢ spoil the countryside...
21 Jonathan:  ⎣ Yeah
22 Marianne:    ... by leaving ...
23 Jonathan:    ... by dropping litter ...
24 Marianne:    ... and broken glass.
```

Qualifying

It will not be necessary to illustrate further the Extending function, since it shades imperceptibly into our next category, the Qualifying function. To add to and extend what someone else has said is inevitably to change it, perhaps to qualify its range of application, or to point out complexities not mentioned in the original statement. Both Extending and Qualifying will unavoidably be illustrated incidentally in many of our quotations, since these moves form the staple of collaborative dialogue. For example, the exchange from Group 1's discussion of 'Work and Energy' was composed mainly of such moves.

Our first example of Qualifying comes from a group and a task which have not previously been mentioned. Groups 9 to 16 are smaller than the other groups, each being composed either of three girls or of three boys. The task in question was related to air pressure, and is called 'Spaceman'. In a previous science lesson a demonstration had been presented to the class in which a corked bottle had been placed inside a bell jar, and the pressure in the bell jar lowered until the cork was ejected from the bottle. The task comprised two questions requiring explanation of the demonstration, and two requiring the pupils to apply the same principle to a spaceship and a spaceman. In the passage to be quoted, Group 16 have gone beyond the task, and have set themselves a new question: they are considering unasked what would have happened if the pressure inside the bottle had been lower than that around it, instead of higher. They had already agreed that the bottle would 'cave in' and continue:

44 Edward:	If it'd been a plastic bottle it would have been erm, crushed in, wouldn't it?	This is the first suggestion that the material of which the bottle is made is likely to affect the outcome.
45 Philip:	Yeah, but it'd have been if it were glass	
46 Harold:	Well, t'glass one would've probably cracked, wouldn't it?	Both take up the idea and apply it to glass
47 Edward:	It, it wouldn't ... If it was thick glass	Dissatisfied with Harold's proposition and wishing to qualify it, raises a new issue, the thickness of the vessel's wall.
	If it was very very thin glass like slide glass ...	Interrupted
48 Harold:	Or't cork would get sucked in	Raises an alternative possibility.
49 Edward:	Or't cork, er. If it was thick glass ...	Accepts Harold's qualification, relating it to the thickness of the glass.
50 Philip:	Yeah t'cork	
51 Harold:	Cork'd get pushed in though, wouldn't it?	Substitutes another formulation for No.48.
52 Philip:	Yeah cork'd also get pushed in then that'd mean that air would have got into the bottle, so it wouldn't have happened.	Attempts to summarise, interrelating what has gone before.
53 Harold:	Most likely cork'd get pushed in, rather than t'jar smashed.	Agreement reached.
54 Edward:	Yeah	

Here the three boys of Group 16 use the talk as an opportunity to interrelate several of the variables which are relevant to explaining the phenomenon considered. They seem to have an intuitive sense of the relevance of the thickness of the vessel's wall, the substance it is made of, and the relation of these to the resistance of the cork, and are through discussion trying to make these explicit in concrete terms. This faces them with considerable

problems of assimilation. For example, when at No.48 Harold puts in
the reference to the cork, Edward might well have treated this
interruption as a threatening contradiction; the momentum of the
discussion however carries the boys on to the point where it has
become clear that Harold's contribution is a qualification not a rejection of what went before, and that it is a useful contribution to
their account.

Similarly in Group 1's discussion of the 'National Parks' task an
apparent contradiction leads the group towards a deeper understanding. In order to deal with the various demands on a National Park
it is useful - and perhaps essential - to define groups of users
with different requirements. This is not immediately obvious to
thirteen-year-olds.

46 Marianne:	At the roadside there should be a lot of big car parks to accommodate all these visitors and tourists.	Proposes facilities for visitors, but fails to make a distinction be-tween different groups of them.
47 David:	Spoil t' countryside, won't it	Points out that these facilities may be in conflict with other requirements.
48 Jonathan:	Ah, that's what'll stop erm, stop em from going all over the countryside, won't it	Suggests that there is no real conflict: the car parks would protect the countryside, not spoil it.
49 David:	That's the big un - to stop people going all over.	Identifies Jonathan's point as the central re-sponsibility of National Parks.
50 Marianne:	But if there's picnic areas. If there's picnic areas then they won't need to go out into the countryside. They'd be able to see it though.	Suggests another device for controlling tourists' use of the Parks.
51 Barbara:	Yeah, but that's it ...	Attempts to enter the discussion.
52 David:	Yeah, but people want to go out into the country-side	Points out that their at-tempt to protect the Parks are ignoring one of their primary purposes, to make the countryside available.

| 53 Marianne: | Not all of em. Just tourists that are passing by ... | Marianne begins to make the necessary distinction between tourists and other users of the National Parks. |

Thus in dealing with particular issues - the provision of car parks and picnic areas - Group 1 have met with differences of opinion which could only be dealt with by moving from the particular issues to more abstract principles, the range of users and their needs. Crucial in this were David's Qualifying move, 'Yeah but people want to go out into the countryside', and Marianne's reception of this, 'Not all of them'; the former showed the group that there was contradiction within what they were saying, and the second showed that a deeper analysis could account for this contradiction. It is worth remembering at this point that these children are thirteen-year-olds of average ability, and that the shift to more abstract levels of analysis illustrated in this example and the previous one represent for them considerable intellectual feats. In both these cases this shift of level depended upon the recognition of contra-dictions, and the willingness to look for principles which would reconcile the contradictions.

In presenting examples of Initiating, Eliciting, Extending and Qualifying moves it has been our intention to show some of the complex skills which younger adolescents command, and which they can under encouraging circumstances utilise in the development of under-standing. These should not be seen merely as individual skills, however: they exist in group discussions or not at all. These moves are mutually supportive: by taking the trouble to elicit an opinion from someone else, or by utilising what has been said by extending it further, the group members ascribe meaningfulness to one another's attempts to make sense of the world. This helps them to continue, however hesitantly, with the attempts to shape their own understanding by talking, and contrasts sharply with any school-ing which reduces the learner to a receiver of authoritative knowledge. It would be misleading, though, not to mention differ-ences of viewpoint. As we have shown earlier in this section, the expression of a dissident opinion, provided it is understood as a qualification and not as a dismissal, plays a crucial part in ad-vances in understanding. The possibility of thus using differences of opinion rests upon a sense of shared validity, and our next section will be devoted to a consideration of the social skills upon which a sense of shared validity depends.

In discussing Collaboration we have been primarily concerned with young people's ability to work together in clarifying their under-standing of a given topic. In the next section we shall be concern-ed with the social skills upon which Collaboration is based, and later with some of the cognitive strategies which the Collaboration makes possible.

2   SOCIAL SKILLS

This section will be concerned with (a) how the given tasks are controlled and carried out, (b) how the group members deal with disagreement and conflict, (c) how they give support and encouragement,
and (d) some more general differences between groups in their behaviour to one another.

For the most part, roles in informal discussion are taken up and
relinquished without this being explicitly acknowledged by the
participants. As we have seen, someone has to propose a topic and
a frame of reference for approaching it; other persons accept this,
or modify it, or put forward an alternative. Sometimes they become
aware of straying from the point and therefore redirect the discussion. Eventually someone will either move the discussion to another topic, or decide that it is concluded. Here we shall necessarily be concerned only with those cases where these choices are
in some sense or other publicly negotiated, though these represent
the exceptions rather than the rule, since for the most part the
discussion is shaped tacitly through the Initiating, Eliciting, Extending and Qualifying moves shown in the last section.

Controlling progress through the tasks

Every group has to control its progress through the given tasks,
determine the boundaries of what is to be considered relevant to
them, and to move at an appropriate moment from one question, or one
aspect of the topic, to another. Where the task includes manipulative activities - as with some of the scientific topics - it is
necessary for one or more members of the group to carry these out.
At the end they have to decide when one member should let the ex-
perimenter know that the discussion is completed.

For the most part, progress through the task is paced by members
of the group reading out another question whenever they feel this to
be appropriate. When pupils do this they are usually not 'playing
the role of the teacher', since unlike teachers they are not asking
questions to which they know the answer in order to test the others'
knowledge. Occasionally the question-asking does approximate to a
different kind of teaching move, that is, when one of the given
questions is used to elicit extended thinking from other members of
the group.

Most of the groups went very deliberately through the 'Spaceman'
questions. Here are the Group 15 boys:

17 Graham:	(The pressure inside the corked bottle) was greater than the pressure outside in the bell jar, so it pushed the, er, cork out.	(Summarised here for brevity) Summarising and complet- ing a sequence.
18 Barry:	Yeah, we did that before just, just before din't we?	Recognising that it was a summary.

19 Graham: Yeah. Number Two: why   Moving on to a new topic
              did the cork come out?   by reading given
                                               question.

              Well we've done that,   Seeking agreement for a
              haven't we?   move on to the third
                                               question.

20 Barry: Yeah we've done that.   Explicit acceptance.
              We've now done two, Tape.   Addresses to the tape
                                               recorder information
                                               about their progress.

It should be made clear that this level of self-awareness was not
common: Barry's last remark suggests that the presence of the tape
recorder may have played some part in this.

Other tasks, however, were not composed of a tightly-structured
series of questions as the 'Spaceman' task was, and this made the
control of relevance a different matter. There was not a great deal
of obvious irrelevance in the discussions of topics such as 'The
Pearl' or 'Vandalism', but the group's attention often moved from
one sub-topic to another without explicit conclusions being formu-
lated. (We are not necessarily regarding this as unhelpful to
learning.) Very occasionally members of the group became aware of
this and attempted to focus the discussion. During their talk about
'The Pearl', for example, Group 1 put forward 'the doctor' as an
example of evil in the story:

    87 David: The doctor were a bit evil though, wan't he?
    88 Barbara: Yeah
    89 Marianne: He's, he's....
    90 David: His big fat, his fat, nose
    91 Barbara: Yeah, I can imagine him
    92 David: ⎡ Yeah, his big fat, his fat and allus smoking big
                   ⎢ cigars and that. He won't, he won't cure anybody.
    93 Marianne: ⎣ Living in towns and that
    94 Marianne: What about the good things, what would you say the
                   good things were?

It seems that Marianne has judged that the discussion of evil had
been satisfactorily concluded, so that it was appropriate to direct
attention to 'the good things'. This was a quotation from the given
task: 'Discuss among yourselves what you have found in the story so
far - the "good and bad things, the black and white things and good
and evil things" as Steinbeck says.' The set task goes on to
mention characters, setting and the way the book is written but
finally to give the pupils the responsibility of deciding what is
worth discussing. In the sequence quoted above Group 1 is guided by
the quotation, though in the discussion as a whole they and the
other groups range widely.

When it comes to ending the whole discussion, groups often reach
agreement by non-verbal signals. In some cases, however, there was
explicit consultation to decide whether they had finished the task:
in ending their discussion of 'Gang Violence' (a variant of the
'Vandalism' task Sheila says, 'I mean, I think we've had enough now
of this so I think we'll tell her eh?' and goes to tell the experi-
menter that they have finished. A more sophisticated version comes

at the end of Group 4's long and exhaustive discussion of 'Steve's
Letter'. Jeanette says, 'Well, I think we've covered all the main
points.' Bill replies 'Yeah', and someone switches off the tape
recorder: they are aware of having completed a successful discussion.

Group 15 were unusually explicit in bringing their two discussions to a conclusion. In the 'Spaceman' task, they had discussed each of the given questions and raised several issues of their
own, when Barry asked, 'I think we've finished now, do you?' There
is some joking about avoiding a lesson, and Alec says:

| 62 Alec: | Erm, shall we go over it again? |
| 63 Barry: | No, we've been through it and all that. We know what happened. |

But Alex insists on recapitulating their answers to the questions
and this takes them on to further discussion of their own about
pressure in the sea. Eventually Graham asks: 'I think we've
finished now, don't you?' and although the others agree they continue talking for a while about a 'pressure pill' in a James Bond
film. Group 15 enjoy talking, and are able to make negotiated decisions about how they do it. In this they contrast markedly with
the girls of Group 9 who went through the questions three times in
a worried search for right answers. But Group 9's difficulties will
provide a topic for a later section.

When a group has not only to control their progress through the
given questions, but also to manipulate materials and apparatus,
allocating tasks to one another, this presents them with special
problems. We shall see later how some groups were almost entirely
prevented from discussion by the requirement to knock holes in egg-
shells. One set of three boys however successfully collaborated in
managing the apparatus upon which the task called 'Carbon Dioxide in
Water' was based.

To understand the social problem (rather than the scientific one)
it is only necessary to know that one member of the group had to
blow into a tube while the others observed the effect of this upon
two containers of lime water. (The boys are Robert and Robin of
Group 3 and Bill of Group 4; they were timetabled together for
science.) Bill begins by claiming the role of blower by saying,
'Right, I'll breathe.' Robert observes what happens and the two of
them discuss what they see. In the course of this Bill moves the
discussion on:

6 Bill:	Now there's the question there. Why does the apparatus only let air in through one tube and only let air out through the other?	Signals change of focus. Quotes question verbatim.
7 Robert:	Well it, it'd suck it, it'd suck it, wun't it?	Attempts an explanation.
8 Bill:	Hold it.	(Difficult to interpret. Perhaps handing over the blowing tube.)

| 9 Robert: | Let's have a look. (Bubbling noises) | Takes on role of blower. |

| 10 Robert: | That's because when you blow through it, it can't .... the air can't .... the air pushes it up in there, dun't it .... the air pushes down on that .... | Attempts an explanation. |

| 11 Bill: | Do it again. | Asks for another opportunity to observe. |

These two boys manage easily to pass the manipulative task to and fro, to decide the sequencing of activities, and to share in explaining. This undoubtedly made easier for them by Robin's willingness to stand back and observe.

Dealing with competition and conflict

In an earlier section we illustrated how the young people in the groups dealt with the need to qualify what others had said, and to accept such qualification of their own statements. When they are able to treat such qualification as a contribution to the group's common thinking and not as a rejection of themselves, no conflict arises. But there are occasions when conflict does arise, and needs to be coped with; here we shall examine only occasions when this is done successfully, leaving failures to a later section.

Group 4 are particularly skilful at dealing with potential social difficulties, and this skill seems to be shared by all four members of the group. Two members of the group have been rapidly drafting an alternative form of 'Steve's Letter', and Alan asks Bill to read his draft, even though he has not completed it.

130 Alan:	What have you got so far, Bill?
131 Jeanette:	Erm, wait a minute, let him finish his first. You read yours, Pauline ['read' is in the present tense].
132 Pauline:	Well, I've put nearly the same as you. [And so on....]

Jeanette manages to head off the interruption to Bill, who is still writing, and instead induces Pauline, who has finished her draft, to read it.

In the next example Group 4 are coping with a substantial difference of opinion. At the beginning of the discussion of 'Steve's Letter', the girls Pauline and Jeanette wish the latter's angry tone to be retained, whereas the boys Bill and Alan want to soften it, because it 'sounds disrespectful', and may prevent future employment. After some discussion they are still divided about this.

| 92 Bill: | If he wants another job I wouldn't put, 'I wouldn't be seen dead in the place.' | Bill wishes to delete one of the more obviously offensive phrases. |

	It's just asking for trouble, in't it?	
93 Alan:	No, it, it's a bit, it's a bit, it's a bit on the....	Trying to frame his objections in moderate terms.
94 Pauline:	Well I don't think he should put so much because really he's just, he's just wanting his attention and say, say ah well he'll give me the job back if I, if I start making trouble for him. He should just put a few words and leave it at that, I think.	Introduces new viewpoint, in effect asking the group to consider the overall purpose of the letter.
95 Bill:	Yeah, well	Message received.
96 Alan:	In some ways I suppose so...	Again a tactful concession of validity to another's views.
97 Bill:	If you put down, if you put down, 'Dear Sir, Thank you for inviting me to this er job....	Sets up an alternative version for ironical purposes.
98 Pauline:	.... but	
97 Bill (cont'd):	but I, I enjoyed it very much'. Well that's telling a complete lie and he's gonna, give you it next year and you're not gonna get any, any more improvements you know.	Makes clear the justification for including an explicit statement of the poor job conditions.
99 Jeanette:	At least he tells the truth.	Reaffirming her original view (that the letter should express the writer's feelings without inhibition).
100 Bill:	Yeah.	
101 Jeanette:	He dun't keep it to himself.	
102 Alan:	I know but he doesn't have to say in that, so many words really.	Concedes validity of Jeanette's views but qualifies them. (Tell

		the truth in a tactful way.)
103 Bill:	No, he could, he could be a bit more res, he could be more respectful.	Agrees with Alan's qualification.
104 Alan:	Yeah, yeah that's, that's more the word, really cos erm, say he might be an old man, a friend like .... (and so on)	Accepts Bill's suggestion, and goes on to put forward a new consideration (the effect of the letter upon the recipient).

This exchange is not untypical of how, in a discussion that is going well, a group will cope with disagreement. It would be a mistake to overemphasise Alan's conciliatory moves, though they may well have played some part in Group 4's exceptional cohesiveness. It is well to note, however, that at least some thirteen-year-olds can work to hold a group together while differences of opinion are being expressed: Alan is not the only member of our groups to make such moves. More important probably is Group 4's willingness to take one another's views seriously even when they disagree with them, and this willingness is clearly demonstrated whenever they counter another opinion with a relevant objection to it, as happens throughout Group 4's discussion of 'Steve's Letter'. It is possible, however, that other groups use gesture and tone of voice to indicate their attentiveness to alternative views. It would be misleading to suggest that this can only be done by verbally explicit means.

To say that Group 4 work well together is not to say that they are mealy-mouthed; in the next exchange, which comes from their 'National Parks' discussion, Alan himself issues a sharp challenge. Alan has suggested that hotels be built for the clubs that use the National Park:

78 Pauline:	Yes, but they don't need these. I mean they can get these anywhere else.
79 Alan:	Why not? Why don't they need them?
80 Pauline:	Well, they don't. I mean this is where they go to....
81 Alan:	Bill, Bill, say if you put hotels - now listen here you - say if these are your hotels, there'll be loads, there'll be loads of people coming won't there? It'll be like a big fairground.

Alan puts his challenge forcefully, and equally forcefully insists that Bill listen to the counter-argument. Yet no personal rejection is implied in the forcefulness; indeed both the challenge and the insistence imply that the others' opinions matter.

We now reach the edge of overt conflict, and this often arises from some boy or girl who has a more aggressive style. Margaret in Group 3 typically asks questions as if she were making an assertion:

16 Margaret:	Hey up, here it says, er National Parks provide er swimming. Why do they want swimming pools then, eh?

Her tone of voice makes this dogmatic assertion, but the group is able to contain her aggressiveness, and later, after a repetition, she has her reply.

    23 Robert: Yeah, well the people, well most people don't like
                  swimming in lakes cos they think they're dirty.
    24 Christine: Yeah, they are.

In a later section we consider occasions when aggressiveness becomes a barrier to the group's engagement with the task.

    Jokes are of considerable importance to all of the groups in coping with strong feelings such as anger and disgust. The 'Bird's Eggs task led to a great deal of joking, Group 5 being particularly inventive:

    'It's gone all over me shoes. I'm only kid in our class with
    yolk-flavoured shoes. Look at em.'

And another member of the group:

    'Somebody's cracked a yolk.'

On some occasions social pressure is put upon group members in a joking manner. Group 4 are discussing 'Work and Energy'; for a while it has been Alan who has carried the main weight of the explaining, with little more than supportive noises from the others, but then they fall silent for several seconds, long enough for them to become aware of a hiatus. Alan, who apparently feels that others should share the responsibility of keeping the talk going, is here far from conciliatory, and breaks the silence by asking in an elaborately artificial voice:

    41 Alan: What do you think of, what do you think about this
                question, Bill? Is work always done when energies
                change in form?

The others laugh loudly, probably appreciating that this is an oblique way of compelling Bill to take more responsibility. Bill replies:

    42 Bill: No not always. It depends what you'd classify as
                work.

And the discussion develops seriously thereafter, with Bill playing a central part in it. Alan has succeeded in manipulating the allocation of social roles without appearing to claim the right to do so, and - as far as one can tell - without giving offence. The possibility of sustained discussion of the topic in hand depends upon allocating roles and responsibilities - an entirely necessary disposition - without spending excessive time upon dispute or decision-making.

Supportive behaviour

It was characteristic of the more successful discussions that members of the groups sometimes asked questions solely in order to bring in contributions from others, either from awareness that they had been silent for a while or from interest in the other's opinion. We are not referring here to initiating moves like those already illustrated, but to those which are addressed to a particular person. The following example comes from Group 4's discussion of 'The Pearl', while they are talking in general terms about their responses to the novel.

    42 Bill: But you've gotta pay, you've gotta pay attention
                to it or you miss something that goes on.

43 Alan: Yeah. What do you think about it, Pauline?
The opening 'Yeah' of Alan's utterance seems to operate as a
'Message received' signal to Bill, so that the coming change of direction will not appear to reject his contribution. Then, aware
that Pauline has not spoken for a while, he tries to bring her in
with an invitation which is in effect a blank cheque to contribute.

A parallel example occurs in Group 1's discussion of 'The Pearl'.
The group has been building up a composite picture of the village
where the events take place when there is a short pause and a change
of direction.

115 Barbara: Go on then, you start ....
116 Marianne: Em, what do you think that'll hap, happen, later
                on in the book when we've read it, you know, what
                will happen to the pearl and the doctor and every-
                thing?
Barbara is willing to step back and give room to Marianne, thus
allowing her to initiate a new strategy which proves to be very
profitable.

We have found no shortage of such moves in those discussions
which have given lengthy attention to the given topic, and would
hypothesise that mutual support of this kind plays an important part
in sustaining attention. It is not merely the acknowledgment of a
common purpose by members of the group: more importantly, when one
replies to another person's remark in careful detail one is assigning significance and validity to it. Even disagreement, if it is
rationally argued and not merely dismissive, will not be interpreted
as aggression by the person to whom it is addressed, but will rather
reinforce his sense of collaborating in the meaningful construction
of knowledge.

The support implicit in attending seriously to another's opinion
may in educational contexts be the form of support most likely to
influence learning. Nevertheless, thirteen-year-old boys and girls
have at their disposal more explicit means of giving support, though
most use them infrequently. (It is worth noting that what we are
calling Social Skills, and especially Supportive Behaviour, are very
poorly represented in Groups 9 to 16, who met only on the one
occasion, in comparison particularly with Groups 1 and 4 who developed a corporate identity.) The means available include the expression of agreement, praise, explicit reference to others' contributions, expressions of positive feeling about what is being
achieved, and naming one another (though naming can be used for
other purposes, as we have seen). In this section we illustrate
these five kinds of supportive behaviour.

Formal expressions of agreement, which are not very common,
appear to occur mainly during the opening moments of discussion,
when all members of the group are eager to encourage fluent talk.
Group 1 begin their discussion of 'National Parks' thus:

1 David: I think that they should put these facilities, er,
                by the roadside and not spoil the countryside, you
                know.
2 Marianne: Yeah, I agree with you.
It seems likely that Marianne is not so much enthusiastic about
David's suggestion as wishing to encourage his initiative in pro-
posing an initial frame of reference. Similarly Group 4's dis-

cussion of 'Work and Energy' begins with a statement by Bill to
which Alan replies:
    4 Alan: Yeah, I agree with you there, Bill.
This is followed by a pause. It seems likely that these expressions
of agreement are useful only when the group have not yet lost their
self-awareness in the talk.

    It is not easy to generalise about naming. The use of Bill's
name by Alan in the above example seems to be part of the rather
self-conscious determination to open lines of communication which
has just been commented on. In the previous section, however, we
looked at an occasion when Alan named Bill in order to persuade him
to take part in the discussion, and our transcriptions contained
another similar example. The importance of naming - when it is not
concerned with forcing participation - is that to address a remark
to someone by name implies an interest in his opinion, which is
likely to encourage a reply. In Group 9, Catherine is talking about
spacemen returning to earth, and wants to enlist the support of
Shirley.
    95 Catherine: They go through a certain space, I don't know how
                   much it is ...
    96 Shirley: What?
    97 Catherine: It presses them down, dun't it, Shirley? It
                   presses em down when they're coming through the
                   air.
    98 Shirley: Mm
Here the naming seems to be part of the appeal for support.

    Sometimes the effect of naming is to imply that disagreement with
another's opinion does not imply a rejection of that person. Here
Group 2 are discussing 'The Pearl':
    52 Sylvia: Yeah, but I suppose if they got a pearl like that
                   they'd spend it on daft things an' all.
    53 Audrey: ⌈ No I don't think so
    54 Sylvia: | I wouldn't be surprised, I wouldn't be surprised
                | if they did
    55 Audrey: ⌊ I don't think so Sylvia
In this case the naming partly performed the function of catching
the attention of the person addressed, but at the same time serves
to express to her an interest in her opinion and its justification.

    As might be expected in informal discussion, explicit reference
back to what another member has said earlier is not common. This is
not to say that they do not take up and utilise others' ideas, both
those which have just been expressed and other ideas from much
earlier in the discussion: most groups do this freely. What we are
concerned with here is the acknowledgment of such indebtedness by an
explicit reference to the source of the opinion, even where it is
referred to in order to be qualified or contradicted. As might be
expected from their display of other social skills Group 4 provide
us with an example, this one from their discussion of the evil
doctor in 'The Pearl':
    22 Alan: It said that er, if you've got some money he'll do
                  it, but if you haven't he won't do it, so he's
                  just after the money really like you said
                  Jeanette.
This reference back to an earlier remark by Jeanette adds little to

the meaning of what is being said, but with other social moves is
important in knitting this group together in defining their responses to the novel.

A contrasting example comes from Group 2's discussion of 'The
Pearl':

60 Audrey: You, you can believe, that, there are people like
                this in the world, and you can believe this story,
                because the way the author, writes it down, the
                way he describes them ....

61 Sylvia: I suppose you've got a point there but erm I don't
                think er, I don't like the village and that that
                it's set in.

The introductory phrase 'I suppose you've got a point there' con-
cedes validity to Audrey's point of view before Sylvia goes on to
express her dislike of the village setting. The softening phrase
is a signal to Audrey that Sylvia values her participation in the
discussion, and does not wish to reject her in voicing an alternative opinion.

Explicit praise of others' contributions is very infrequent
indeed, though Group 4 provide an example. Pauline has just said
that if hotels are provided in National Parks they should not be so
frequent as to 'litter it up', and Bill responds: 'Yeah, that a,
that's a good idea.' Such ready appreciation of others' suggestions
plays its part in sustaining Group 4's exceptional ability to stay
with a topic, exploring it from various points of view.

One would expect that any group thus committed to collaborative
discussion would support themselves with expressions of shared
feeling. Several groups expressed satisfaction at what they had
achieved by the end of their discussion. It is Group 1 who express
most clearly their empathy with one another; and especially during
their discussion of 'The Pearl' which clearly gave them pleasure.
This satisfaction is twice expressed by David, first in appreciation
of the recreation by Marianne of part of the story.

98 Marianne: But the writer keeps mentioning in the story about
                the music that comes into Kino's ears, dun't he?
                You know, the family music and then it's the evil
                music that comes when, when the scorpion's there,
                it's evil music playing in his ears. I think I
                like that, you know.

99 David: Shuper
The relish with which David re-experiences Steinbeck's metaphor is
richly embodied in his tone of voice, so that the listener is aware
of a warmth with which this group are able to share the recollected
experience. And at the end of the discussion he sums up the group's
sense of a job well done with the same word 'Super'.

Collaborating or defending

Our concern lies not with social skills for their own sake but only
with the extent to which they contribute to a group's ability to
learn from discussion. Each group is simultaneously negotiating
social relationships and attempting the given task: if the former
pre-empts their time and attention, little learning will go on.

For this reason we have wished to understand how the young people
cope with social relationships, and with the allocation of roles,
and therefore with the allocation of power over the progress of the
discussion. No doubt much of this negotiation goes on through intonation, facial expression and bodily posture and gestures: in
focussing attention upon those social moves which are put into
words, we are implicitly treating these as representative of the
other less accessible moves, and may therefore be misrepresenting
the whole. It may well be, for example, that when a group is
smoothly constructing an interpretation of the given task, there is
no need for relationships to be negotiated explicitly. Therefore,
we wish in this section to consider the group's social strategies
more generally.

   To distinguish a productive from a defensive approach to a task
we next compare exchanges from two groups' discussion of the 'Causes
of Vandalism' task. (They had been given extracts from a transcribed interview with Ron, the former leader of a boys' gang, and were
asked in general terms to discuss the causes of gang violence and
vandalism. This should be distinguished from the variant of this
task - called 'Gang Violence' - given to Groups 9 to 16.) In both
cases the exchange quoted comes from near the beginning of the
recording; they have been chosen not for the content of what is
said, but to illustrate the difference in the two groups' approaches. The first example comes from Group 1:

3 David:	I think the area you live in er, could affect the way they behave because when there's other gangs around you, I think it er, you know make you want to fight too. If you see em all, fighting and that, it looks like fun and so he'll just join in.	An initiating move to start the discussion. Links the general issue with the particular case of Ron.
4 Jonathan:	Yeah, he only, only, he'll only start fighting if other people do.	Accepts David's lead and extends it.
5 Marianne:	And he thinks that the only way he can make his self, big, and make his self a somebody, is to prove to people that he is, big and is, tough and fight, and can fight all the time.	Further extends this line of thought by reminding the group of Ron's need for self-display.
6 David:	Well he wan't, he wan't very tough at school war he and no, nobody like....	Both David and Marianne are inventing realistic supportive detail, none of which is given in the task materials.

7 Marianne:	No, his parents, his parents were always hitting him	
8 David:	Nobody liked him did they, so he wanted to make him-self right big by beating everybody up, so he'd be famous.	Further extending the construction of Ron's motives.
9 Marianne:	And he in't really brainy so he had to do it in a different way .... (etc.)	Qualifying the foregoing with a further insight.

In this exchange we have no explicit supportive moves of the kinds discussed above, but instead close attentiveness to what has gone before, so that each utterance is closely linked to its prede-cessors. This becomes partly overt in the linking phrases, 'Yeah, he only ...', 'And he thinks ...', 'Well, he wan't ...' and so on, but more significant is the closeness with which the content of each utterance is related to what has preceded it.

In contrast to this let us look at Group 3's approach to the same task. Robert has begun by rejecting the idea that young people engage in vandalism because they 'aren't given enough things to do'.

5 Robert:	Oh I, I don't, I, I think its partly that, but you get some people that, really want to be vandals really want to smash things up just for't pleasure of it, and you get some that an't owt better to do so they just go around smashing things up.	Puts forward two parallel explanations.
	It's a bit daft really in't it...?	Invites others to join in.
6 Christine:	Say summat Margaret (Whispered)	Primarily concerned with whether the other girl is doing a fair share.
7 Margaret:	You an't said owt yet (Whispered)	As above.
8 Christine:	I've said 'Yeah', 'Yeah'. (Whispered)	As above.
9 Robert:	Do you think Ron's any good?	Tries to initiate a new strategy.
10 Christine:	No	A minimal response.

11 Margaret:	Do you think Ron's what?	Aggressive tone: sounds like a refusal to contribute.
12 Christine:	He dun't give, he dun't give good answers.	Tries to respond to Robert's initiating move (No.9).
13 Robert:	No, he just said that he wanted to be 'somebody'. He could have been somebody if he worked hard couldn't he, instead of...	Extends Christine's response by making it more specific. Interrupted.
14 Margaret:	Yeah but not like that	?
15 Robert:	Instead of, he always wanted to make people be frightened of him.	Completing his previous contribution.

Although this is a topic about which most adolescents have plenty to say, Group 3 - for one reason or another - are making little progress. Robert is trying to get the discussion going, while the two girls block his attempts by squabbling or by refusing to accept his leads or (later in the recording) by making fun. The other boy joins in later, but only when forced to do so by one of the girls. (Later in the discussion Robert too does not listen to the others and interrupts them, ignoring their contributions and failing to address them or ask them for elucidation.) Perhaps they suffer from shyness, or do not like one another, or resent being recorded, or are not interested in the subject, or dislike school; the reasons for their failure to work together need not concern us at this moment. In contrast with Group 1, they are not attending closely to one another, there is no sense of common purpose, and no sign of encouragement, but rather of aggression and self-protection. If these three are usefully to take part in group discussion it will be necessary to involve them in finding a topic and a social context that is meaningful to them. Our intention here, however, is to contrast with our example of collaborative discussion another example in which the young people showed too much distrust of one another and the context to find collaboration possible. It is unlikely that the members of Group 3 lack the social skills that we have been looking at, but here and in the other recordings they did not use them as frequently as did Groups 1 and 4. They seem to be too concerned with some potential threat to their integrity or self-respect to be able to take the risks necessary if they are to participate in exploratory talk of this kind, at least in this context. Confidence in oneself and trust of others seem to be a necessary condition for it. As one would expect, we found such confidence and trust more commonly in those groups who worked together for some months in making recordings than in those whom we brought together only once. (This was not, however, true of Group 3.) But that is a topic for a later section.

3 COGNITIVE STRATEGIES

Collaboration, however, is not enough: the talk must lead to the
construction of new ways of understanding. In this section we
attempt to display some of the strategies of thought that our groups
were able to use in trying to make sense of the tasks given to them.
In analysing systematically the range of logical relationships which
might link an utterance to its predecessors we found examples of the
following:

1   Proposes a cause
2   Proposes a result
3   Expands loosely (e.g. descriptive details)
4   Applies a principle to a case
5   Categorises
6   States conditions under which statement is valid or invalid
7   Advances evidence
8   Negates
9   Evaluates
10 Puts alternative view
11 Suggests a method
12 Restates in different terms

This list may well not be exhaustive, since the logical relationships used clearly depend upon the given task; in 'Work and
Energy', for example, there were many examples of No.4, Applies a
principle to a case, whereas in 'Causes of Vandalism' there were
many examples of No.3, Expands loosely. Most of these twelve
logical relationships can easily be identified in the examples given
in previous sections, so that there would be little value in illus-
trating them individually. Moreover, such categories do not prove
in practice very useful in identifying the precise way in which a
group develops a line of thought. If you turn back to Group 1's
discussion at the beginning of this chapter and look at the way each
utterance expands what goes before, you will find a wide range of
relationships, none of which exactly fits the categories of our
list. Thus, in order to understand how a group constructs
knowledge, we find it more valuable to use a descriptive approach.
    Instead of using those logical categories therefore, we shall
illustrate in this section how members of a group construct the
question that they are to answer, raise new questions of their own,
set up hypotheses, use evidence and express feelings and recreate
experience. We shall call these the 'cognitive strategies' adopted
by the group.

Constructing the question

It would be a mistake to think that when the set task, typed on
cards, has been put into the hands of the boys and girls in a group
that they yet 'know what the question is'. To turn the typed words
into something which can be answered it is necessary for members of
the group to 'construct the question', by using what they know already to make sense of it. In some cases, our groups had already in

lessons spent some time in clarifying the issues - especially in the
science tasks 'Work and Energy' and 'Spaceman' - yet they were still
left with problems of definition. Here is the beginning of Group
4's attempt at 'Work and Energy':

1 Bill:	There's no work involved in electricity to light a light bulb
2 Jeanette:	No, I don't think so.
3 Bill:	Unless erm, unless you erm, involve the work of the men in the turbine station that produces the electricity to make the light.

The 'Work and Energy' task with its tight definitions of those two
concepts might at first glance seem to leave the group with nothing
to do but to apply these definitions to the given examples. But no
definitions can be as tight as that, for the definitions themselves
have to be interpreted. In this example, Bill seems to be facing
two problems as he tries to use the teacher's conceptual scheme as
a tool of thinking:

(a) separating the technical meaning of 'work' from the everyday
     concept ('the work of the men in the turbine station')
(b) determining the limits of the given example ('Electricity to
     light a light bulb'), that is, whether it includes the
     generation of the electricity.

The first of these is a familiar problem in science teaching; it is
noteworthy that Bill is still not clear about 'work' in spite of the
discussion in the lesson. The second was quite unexpected, for the
questioner had taken this boundary as self-evident. However clearly
the teacher frames his exposition or chooses his questions the
learner must use what he knows already in order to make sense of
them. In the groups we are able to observe this happening; in
other lessons it must go on silently, if at all.

The construction of the question is a different matter in non-
scientific topics such as 'Causes of Vandalism' and 'The Pearl'.
Neither the boundaries of the task nor the concepts to be used have
been sharply defined. The pupils are not faced with the problem of
projecting themselves into the teacher's conceptual scheme; instead
they must construct one for themselves. In these cases, the construction of questions may form the predominant part of the discussion, and be indistinguishable from the construction of answers.
Since the progressive definition of the problem - or problems - goes
on throughout the discussion it is diffuse and therefore difficult
to illustrate, but two sections from the beginning of Group 2's 'The
Pearl' discussion will give some impression. It will be remembered
that the task gave the young people a very open brief to discuss
good and evil in the story. They begin thus:

2 Audrey:	In, in this book I think it's trying to get through to you that money, is evil, and when you possess money you tend, you tend to, to teck, to take it for granted and then, buy things and spend it.
3 Sylvia:	Spend it on anything that you just fancy that's in fashion probably what we do

Out of the many moral issues which they might have chosen they have

in fact gone to one of the novel's major themes, though here they
state it in terms of their own experience. As they develop the
theme, however, it becomes more closely focussed upon the issues
which are presented in the novel.

13 Sylvia:	And you probably think that what Kino's spending when he gets that, when he sells pearl and gets money for that we'll probably think you know getting married, spending t'money on getting married when they're already, living together and that ...	Relates idea of self-indulgent spending to the novel, not in terms of what 'would happen' but as a hypothetical reader's response to the events.
14 Arthur:	They, they - all the people round table, they says that, er, they'd spend it on charities but Kino and his wife says they're gonna spend it on erm, on theirselves	Focusses the issue of appropriate spending by using an episode in the novel.
15 Sylvia:	Yes	
16 Paul:	I bet, I bet they'd all spend it on their sens. I mean, I bet they wun't spend it on charities and all that, they'd spend it on their sens [i.e. themselves].	Questions whether Kino's neighbours, 'the people round the table', would in real life do what they advise Kino to do - which is an appropriate interpretation of that episode.
17 Sylvia:	I wouldn't spend it on charities	Relating novel to their own motives. Takes the interpretation of the episode one step further.
18 Audrey:	I know I wouldn't ... I mean, the people in the village know that Kino and his wife are going to spend it silly, and not give it to worthwhile causes.	

What seems to be happening in the whole episode - both before and
after this extract - is that the group are sharpening their focus
upon two parallel issues. One is the question of what is a morally
defensible way of spending a large windfall of money; the other is
how to interpret the beahviour and attitudes of 'all the people
round the table', that is the neighbours who speak of what they
would do if they had found the pearl.
     In describing this kind of discussion as 'constructing questions'
we do not mean that the young people necessarily formulate them as

questions - though sometimes they do, as we have shown. It is
rather that a discussion of this more open kind is made up of
a series of attempts to arrive at a shared framework such that
after a while some contributions will seem relevant, and others
will seem irrelevant or changes of subject. This building up of
a framework of relevance is more obviously present in more open
discussions, but is nevertheless going on in all of them. In some
of the topics, such as 'Work and Energy', they construct this
framework with half an eye on the teacher's intentions, and are attempting to conform to what they believe to be his view of what is
relevant.

Raising new questions

It was in the nature of this study that in setting the task we
should follow the wishes of the teachers we were collaborating
with. This has meant that in some tasks the attention of the pupils
was tightly structured by a series of questions, and that in others
they were more free to find issues for themselves. In this section
is illustrated the way in which our thirteen-year-olds are able to
move outside the given framework and ask useful questions of their
own, all three of the examples being taken from discussions of the
'Spaceman' topic where the tightly-framed set questions make it easy
to recognise when the pupils raise issues of their own.
    The three boys of Group 16 had given a very competent explanation
of why the cork was expelled from the bottle when the pressure
outside it had been lowered. Then suddenly, in the midst of this
discussion, one of them considered as a hypothetical possibility the
reversal of the relative pressure so that the pressure was greater
outside the bottle.

29 Philip:	If it'd been put other way round it'd, it'd have ...	Raises new possibility. (Interrupted.)
30 Edward:	Well it was, it was wan't it?	Misunderstanding?
31 Philip:	No I mean if ...	Attempts to explain.
32 Harold:	Yeah	Supports Edward.
33 Philip:	No, I mean if there was air on the outside, and not in the bottle it'd just ...	Expands his own earlier contribution (No.29).
34 Edward:	Nowt would have happened	Dismisses the hypothetical case.
35 Philip:	It would	
36 Harold:	It'd cave in, wouldn't it?	Harold now sees the point.

37 Philip:	It'd cave in. Cos if there's no pressure on the bottle	Attempts to justify his assertion.
38 Harold:	It'd crush it wouldn't it?	Completes Philip's explanation.
39 Philip:	... no pressure forcing out of the bottle ... (and so on)	Rephrases.

The two boys, Harold and Philip, have explored this counter-possibility, and Edward joins in later. In the preceding exchanges Edward had dominated the discussion: this may explain his initial failure to understand Philip's suggestion, and his attempt to dismiss it. The egocentric desire to display knowledge is frequently in effective opposition to the wish to collaborate in constructing knowledge. The alternative case which Philip has put forward has given the group a useful opportunity to test their grasp of the underlying principle. The task, however, had not suggested to them that they should try other possible cases.

To take another example, when the boys of Group 15 discuss the final question of the 'Spaceman' task (that is, what would happen to a man if he went outside a space ship without a space suit), members of the group raise a series of new topics. They have agreed that the man would explode, and Barry asks:

30 How does a pace, space suit stop it? Is there air inside?
A few moments later Barry compares a space suit to a diving suit, and then asks:

41 I wonder how fish and all them survive down there then.
Later they discuss why flat fish are flat. They are able to extrapolate from what they have learnt, and indeed are eager to integrate and interrelate this with a wide range of knowledge which they already have. In comparison, the given topic, in its attempt to encourage explicit explanation and a thorough grasp of the principles involved, fails to ask for some relevant understanding which these boys possess.

The girls of Group 12, although they approach the 'Spaceman' questions systematically and with serious intentions, display some lack of grasp of the concept of pressure when they are working within the framework given to them. But one of them shows herself able to criticise the assumptions upon which one of the questions is based, the question which asks, 'If a piece of rock hit a spaceship and made a hole in it, what would happen to the air inside?'

30 Nicola:	Also if a spaceship is up in't, you know, up in't air, up in't, you know, space and there's no air around and the rock is floating about, the rock down, down, you know, you know, on the land level would be heavy.
31 Teresa:	Yeah
32 Nicola:	But up, you know, past gravity and that ...
33 Teresa:	Yeah, it's light as a sponge
34 Nicola:	It'll be, it'll be, it'll be ve, it'll be light as

a sponge. So I think that's really a daft
question because I don't think a rock in space
could, you know, force a hole in a spaceship.

Nicola has misinterpreted statements about the 'weightlessness' of
objects in a moving spaceship to imply that at a distance from the
earth objects are 'past gravity' (i.e. beyond the reach of gravity),
and therefore have no mass. This idea she transfers to a piece of
rock coming from elsewhere, deducing that it will be 'light as a
sponge' and that it therefore will lack the momentum to pierce the
metal skin of a spaceship. Within the bounds of her current understanding of the phenomena, Nicola is reasoning with commendable
ingenuity and consistency, and making a useful effort to relate
the set question to her understanding of the behaviour of masses in
space. Her criticism of the question is a mark of her awareness
that the two do not match. Unfortunately the girls do not pursue
this issue further.

A similar flexibility in raising new questions was shown in the
discussion based on other topics, and especially by Groups 1 to 4,
who became more habituated to working in groups. Both 'The Pearl'
and 'National Parks' in their very nature required the young people
to select their own frames of reference, and their ability to do so
has already been illustrated in the section concerned with Initiating Moves. The tightly structured series of questions used in
certain topics probably helped the groups to achieve concentration
and clarity, but may have impeded them from relating the new
knowledge to what they already knew. For teaching purposes there
might have been some value in appending to the set questions an
invitation to raise doubts, pursue new examples, suggest new issues
and so on.

Setting up hypotheses

In the nature of things most of the contributions put forward by
members of the groups were hypothetical, at least in the sense that
they involved going beyond the given information in setting up an
explanation or an interpretation. A convenient example comes from
the end of Group 4's discussion of 'The Pearl'.

123 Pauline: I wonder what made him write such a story
124 Bill: Probably erm, thought that the plight of these
               sort of people was worth writing about so that
               they'd erm, so that everybody would know what it
               was like to live in a village and feel a bit sorry
               for em, you know.

The deliberate attempt to build an explanation up out of hints and
impressions leads them towards a valuable insight.

What we are concerned with here, however, are explicit hypotheses, where a boy or girl sets up an alternative possibility in order
to explore how it would work. These often arose as implicit ways of
testing the generality of explanations used to account for the given
case, but not always. Our first example is a simple one. Alan
begins Group 4's discussion of 'Steve's Letter' with the hesitant
assertion, 'I don't think you'd write that to yer, yer best mate or
yer friend would yer', but a few speeches later Pauline retorts:

      7 Pauline: Yeah, but he might not be a best friend
      8 Alan: Eh no, just, just say if it was ... (and so on)
Pauline is perfectly right to doubt whether Steve's employer is
likely to be his best friend, yet Alan has a good reason for insist-
ing that the implications of that possibility should be explored,
since a moment later he reaches the important insight that an appropriate style would depend on the person addressed. (This may
seem obvious to the reader, but it was not in the least obvious to
these thirteen-year-olds.) The next two contributions ran in fact
thus:
      9 Pauline: Well it's his boss, in't it?
     10 Alan: He, he'd put different things, wouldn't he? It
                      depends who he's writing to really.
Thus this minor - and apparently unrealistic - hypothesis led to a
significant contribution to the discussion.
     We have already seen how Group 16 tested their explanation of why
the cork was ejected from the bottle by considering what would have
happened had the bottle been made of plastic, of thin or of thick
glass, and then by discussing what would have happened had the
greater pressure been outside, instead of inside, the bottle. This
testing against hypothetical cases did not seem to be a deliberate
technique, but to be put forward piecemeal by members of the group,
as they thought of cases which it would be interesting to consider.
When teachers are guiding group discussion by work sheets similar to
our task cards, they would, in our opinion, be well advised to encourage pupils to go beyond the set questions by raising issues of
their own, and, if it is possible, by finding ways of investigating
these. Many of our thirteen-year-olds proved quite capable of
improvising ideas and strategies, once they realised that these were
acceptable. Too strict a schedule of questions may persuade pupils
that their own thinking is not wanted.

Using evidence

In any learning the learners have to utilise what they already know
in order to give meaning to new insights or information which they
are given. New understanding is likely to be a reorganisation of
old knowledge rather than an addition to it. Thus an essential
cognitive strategy is the ability to utilise previous knowledge and
experience to throw light upon the matter in hand. This section is
concerned both generally with the young people's use of their existing knowledge as a resource, and with their more explicit use of
information in the testing of general assertions.
     It was the two tasks relating to violence amongst adolescent boys
which most obviously invited the groups to utilise their everyday
knowledge. Group 9 began their 'Gang Violence' discussion with:
     Catherine: Well if you remember when we went to London,
                     Elizabeth, when, you know, in the Tube Station
                     (Yeah) there were lots, we saw people with bottles
                     and that, and knives, that's because there's a
                     football match on and I suppose this is the
                     difference because, one supports one team and one
                     supports, another and if you remember ... (and so
                     on)

Such direct use of first-hand anecdote was infrequent, however, and
may only have occurred here because Catherine and Elizabeth are
sisters. More commonly in the 'Gang Violence' and 'Causes of
Vandalism' topics the boys and girls used their first-hand
knowledge - which in some cases seemed extensive - to build up typical cases of violence, or to characterise typical gang members and
their motives. Here is Group 4 ('Causes of Vandalism'):

17 Alan: They've nowt to do so they say, 'Come on we'll
               stir up a bit of trouble'.
18 Bill: Yeah, it starts off as a bit of fun, you know,
               sort of a pretend fight.
19 Alan: It starts off wi' their fists and somebody gets
               rough.
20 Bill: Yeah
21 Alan: And somebody uses a bottle or chains or hammers,
               summat like that.
22 Pauline: Yeah
23 Jeanette: Yeah, and they do it for no reason at all.
24 Bill: Well it depends doesn't it ... (and so on)

Their strategy for discussing the cause of violence is to utilise
their background knowledge to construct a hypothetical case which
can thereafter be used as a basis for explicit generalisation. The
hypothetical case itself is an implicit generalisation; although it
is made up of concrete details these are implicitly held to be
general. This can be seen as a special case of the strategy described above as 'constructing the question': it is as if the group
had found the interview with the gang-leader, Ron, to be an inadequate basis for a discussion of motives and had therefore suppli-
ed far more data in the form of typical cases. On the basis of this
data they can then go on to deal explicitly with the question of
motives: Jeanette in the extract above makes an explicit generalisation, 'They do it for no reason at all', which provokes Bill to
question the generality of her statement:

24 Bill: Well it depends doesn't it. There may be two or
               three gangs going around and if somebody wants to,
               there may be just one discoteque and with two or
               three gangs it gets a bit crowded so everybody
               loses their temper and then it starts off with
               fists and then turns into a full-scale rumble, a
               fight and that.

Bill is questioning the generality of Jeanette's statement not by
another explicit generalisation but by putting forward another and
different typical case, which is itself an implicit generalisation.
It is important to notice that although much of the discussion of
these two topics is conducted in all the groups through hypothetical
cases this does not mean that these thirteen-year-olds are incapable
of generalised thinking about social issues. Indeed, their hypothetical cases, which might at a glance be dismissed as low-level
'concrete' thinking, function as generalisations. The use of an
example is certainly not blocking them off from access to contradictory examples or - as Bill shows - from awareness of the general
principles implicit in the examples.

It is not only in the more open topics that the groups utilise
knowledge from everyday life. In 'Work and Energy' it is not possi-

ble to apply the definitions of 'work' and 'energy' to examples without using everyday knowledge about steam engines, light bulbs, and so on. Bill is once again particularly successful in linking school concepts with his everyday knowledge:

29 Bill: Although you could erm, connect something to the steam engine, so you could have heat to movement in the steam engine, the steam engine connected by pulley to a turbine, producing electricity to light a light bulb.

This witty display of how the two examples of change of form of energy given in the task could be joined by a string of changes is exceptional. Similar links between the tasks and everyday life were made by all the groups: indeed the questions could hardly be discussed without using knowledge of how things are in the world.

So far 'evidence' has been used loosely to refer to the bringing-in of knowledge from outside the school. Yet thirteen-year-olds are capable of using evidence in the stricter sense, that is, of deliberately adducing arguments to support or disprove a general assertion. We have already quoted the end of Group 1's discussion of the verisimilitude of Steinbeck's 'The Pearl', and now turn for our example to the beginning of that episode.

34 David:	Well I, the best part I liked were, when, when he went looking for the pearl down in't sea, did you?	Initiates new focus with expression of approval.
35 Marianne:	Yeah it should have des, - had a bit more description about the actual diving	Accepts the focus but qualifies the approval with a criticism.
36 Barbara:	Yes, of the sea	Offers an anternative version of the criticism.
37 David:	Yeah	
38 Marianne:	Because, if, if he's supposed to be a diver he han't spent much time, diving has he?	Offers evidence to support the general assertion.
39 David:	He just went down and it were there waiting for him, wan't it?	Extending Marianne's contribution, adding further evidence.
40 Marianne:	He should have had to search for it first.	Further extending.
41 Barbara:	It seems a bit funny that as soon as baby gets hurt ...	Offers different evidence to support Marianne's assertion.
42 Marianne:	That he should find the pearl.	Completes Barbara's contribution.

In this exchange, Group 1 without any prompting turn to their
memories of the text to find supporting evidence, since it is clear
that all three have at one point or another found this part of the
novel unrealistic (as it is intended to be). Such references to
incidents of the novel were common in several groups' discussions
of 'The Pearl'. We have already illustrated several occasions when
a sceptical boy or girl has asked another for supporting evidence,
for example Louise's 'What makes you think so?' in Group 5's 'Bird's
Eggs' which we quoted as an example of 'Eliciting'. Whereas for the
most part the bringing forward of evidence to support or challenge
assertions is done by normal Extending or Qualifying moves, there
are occasions when the group members quite explicitly ask for
evidence or supply it. Although for the most part the construction
of knowledge is carried on intuitively, without reflection, when
necessary the production of evidence can represent a deliberate and
conscious strategy. The theme of reflective and conscious strategies will be developed later.

Expressing feelings and recreating experience

Not all of the topics discussed in the groups were so separate from
what mattered in the young people's lives that they could withdraw
from commitment and discuss them with the detachment which (perhaps
wrongly) is often held to be 'academic'. Some topics came close
enough to a boy's or girl's own concerns to call forth expressions
of feeling. These should be distinguished from the expressions of
feeling towards one another which were as likely to be generated
during detached topics as during those concerned with urgent issues.
With the expression of feeling about the topic we are linking the
recreation of remembered responses to literature, since it is a
characteristic of a good story to strike a spark of sympathetic
feeling in the reader, even when the events of the story are concerned with such distant people as Mexican pearl-fishers.

One might have expected the 'Causes of Vandalism' topics to
generate feelings, but those were on the whole treated as something
that happened to someone else, even though these persons were often
claimed as acquaintances. Expressions of feeling occurred frequently during the discussion of 'Life in the Trenches', a task which we
have not had occasion to mention before. In previous lessons a
teacher had presented to the class a variety of information about
the First World War. This had included a film, and examples of
letters and publications of the period. Besides this, the pupils
were probably able to call on other information from television
programmes and elsewhere. The task required the pupils to discuss
life in the trenches during the war, stressing the soldiers' experience of danger and discomfort. A few utterances from Group 7 can
represent many of the expressions of feeling generated by what they
had seen and heard.

94 Mary:	And so many people get killed a day don't they, quite a lot of people? Yeah
95 Dorothy:	Yeah and if, if I were there erm ...
96 Gordon:	Oh I don't know
97 Dorothy:	I'd hate it if any of me good pals got killed or owt

        98 Gordon: Got killed
        99 Mary: Yeah, I know
       100 Dorothy: It's horrible, you see em all dying on't picture
                       though
       101 Mary: Mm
The common feeling generated in the group is patent even in transcription, and it is clearly most relevant to the topic which they
are discussing.
     It would have been difficult to predict, however, what one boy
said during such a discussion in Group 6:
        12 Carl: It was daft wan't it?
        13 Paula: What were?
        14 Carl: That First World War
        15 Paula: What d'you mean it were daft?
        16 Trevor: All bloody wars are daft aren't they?
Whatever Carl's original remark meant it gave Trevor an opportunity
to express with some force what we would interpret as a general
judgment. It is well to remember that thirteen-year-olds live in a
moral world, part of which they have clearly mapped so that they can
make certain moral judgments with clarity and warmth. It might
perhaps be added that Trevor's contribution shows yet another form
of knowledge which may be brought into school, an ethical principle
very different from the particular cases discussed above under the
heading 'Using Evidence'.
     In the previous section we showed Group 1 criticising parts of
'The Pearl' for a lack of verisimilitude. This criticism did not,
however, negate their very real appreciation of the novel. Marianne
has asked for more description of 'the actual diving', and in reply
David reminds the group of part of the diving which had been told in
detail. (Part of this has previously been quoted for another
purpose.)
        59 David: Well when he came ... Well they described that how
                      long he held his breath. When, when he came up
                      and when he, when he slipped a knife into it [i.e.
                      the oyster], it tightened up and he couldn't open
                      it.
        60 Marianne: Mm, that were good.
        61 David: And when, when he did eventually open it, er, he
                      said, the pearl were as big as erm ...
        62 Marianne: As his hand. It just laid in his hand, din't it?
Rehearsing the incident has recreated for these two their own remembered enjoyment in reading the episode. Marianne's tone as she
says, 'As his hand. It just laid in his hand, din't it?' expresses
the relish she feels at the image of the enormous pearl. Such recreation of response to the story was not uncommon in the discussions of 'The Pearl', though the explicit 'Mm, that were good'
might be difficult to match from another group.
     It is important not to restrict 'the construction of knowledge'
so that it applies only to knowledge distant from the knower's own
concerns, since our most important knowledge is not of that kind.
The knowledge which bears directly on children's daily lives, and
on which they base their actions, has its own part to play in school
learning, and it is well not to forget this.

4 REFLEXIVITY

As we have seen, the adolescents in our sixteen groups collaborate
in sequential and meaningful talk, manage their social relationships, and adopt rational strategies in coping with the tasks. But
how far are they aware of doing all these things? How far can they
monitor their own behaviour so as to adjust and modify their strategies? Piaget's studies of young people's cognitive development
would lead one to expect that our average thirteen- to fourteen-
year-olds, given familiar subject-matter and helpful circumstances,
would be reaching out towards the more reflective forms of thought
which characterise what Piaget calls the formal operational stage
of development. One would expect them to be able occasionally to
see their own viewpoint as one amongst several possible ones, and
to relate under overarching principles their own and other people's
viewpoints; to be able to set up hypothetical explanations and to
test them; to be able to evaluate their own and others' viewpoints,
treating them as open to modification; and to be consciously choosing both the cognitive strategies used, and some of the social
skills. Some of these characteristics of hypothetico-deductive
thinking we have already illustrated in earlier sections, but here
we are particularly concerned with self-awareness and the monitoring
of one's own strategies. Since they depend upon the ability to reflect upon one's thinking, we deal with these characteristics
together here under the heading of 'reflexivity'.
   In this section we consider the monitoring by the young people
of their own speech and thought strategies, their ability to
interrelate alternative viewpoints, their evaluating of their own
and others' performances, and their awareness of the group's strategies. Finally we note that there are circumstances under which
reflexivity is not necessary.

Monitoring their thinking

We begin with some examples which show at a very simple level that
one of the young people is listening to what he is saying and evaluating it. This becomes clear when one of them corrects himself in
mid-sentence, aware that what he is saying will be understood in
ways that do not match his intentions. Alec in Group 15, for
example, is explaining why the cork comes out in the 'Spaceman' task
when he realises that he has not said what he intended:
   8 Alec: There's an even pressure on the bottle which let,
               keeps the cork on.
He seems to have begun to say that equal pressure inside and outside
the bottle would 'let' the cork stay in place, and then to have
realised that this carries unwanted associations of giving per-
mission to a human being, so that he hastily substitutes 'keeps'.
   A more important kind of self-awareness is shown by Bill when
Group 4 are talking about water in their 'Work and Energy' discussion:

   20 Alan: It moves down stream and   Applying the concept of
                 it, it turns, turbines to   change of energy to the

	make electricity and it can use it to be a water mill as well.	movement of water downhill.
21 Bill:	That could be a follow on, you could say erm, water to turbine, turbine to, to erm, energy, energy to electricity to light in a light bulb.	Attempts a systematic analysis of the changes in energy linking falling
	You could say that couldn't you?	Checks that Alan would accept this formulation.

Here we interpret the repeated phrase 'could say' as showing that Bill regards his analytical account not as absolute but as an interpretation open to later modification. That is, he is aware of taking part in the construction of knowledge, and - appropriately - regards that knowledge as provisional. We have already quoted (in the section 'Using evidence') an occasion from the 'Causes of Vandalism' discussion in which Bill uses the phrase 'Well, it depends, doesn't it?' to indicate that he wishes two alternative accounts to be considered together: this seems to show an analogous pattern of thought.

Many of the examples put forward in the last section under the headings of 'Raising new questions' and 'Setting up hypotheses' depend equally on the ability to hold simultaneously several alternative possibilities and to follow their implications. This can also be linked with the more self-conscious demands for evidence, such as David's 'Well where's the force?' in Group 1's discussion of 'Work and Energy'. Such awareness of evidence provides the young people with a method for evaluating the alternative possibilities.

Relating alternative constructions

The ability to treat viewpoints as hypothetical carries with it the possibility of according validity to others' views even when they clash with one's own. The following may be primarily a tactful gesture which we might have used in the section on Social Skills to illustrate how one of the girls is able to soften her disagreement by acknowledging the validity of the opinion she is contradicting. On the other hand it could equally be an acknowledgment that the other's suggestion makes sense in its own terms. Group 4 are discussing whether buildings such as restaurants should be allowed in National Parks. One of the boys thinks that such buildings, if surrounded by trees, would be acceptable.

18 Alan:	Yeah, but I think you could have all these buildings if they were specially camouflaged. Say you build your restaurants, and you have the opened - and your front, with the front on to the road and trees surrounding it.
19 Pauline:	Yeah but even that ...
20 Alan:	You know, big trees so you wouldn't be able to

see it, you know, so it would not, wouldn't spoil
the view.

21 Jeanette: Yeah, you could look at it like that. I think
these things that are in towns, like nightclubs
and casinos are going to spoil it.

It is not easy to determine the meaning of Jeanette's 'You could
look at it like that'. It is certainly of social value in ensuring
that the contrary view she is about to express does not destroy the
group's sense of a common direction. At the same time, it seems
likely to be an acknowledgment that Alan's argument about concealing
the buildings is persuasive: here the cognitive and the social go
hand in hand.

In Group 1 Marianne provides rather different evidence of using
the deliberate strategy of holding more than one viewpoint in mind
during a discussion. In their 'National Parks' discussion David
reminds the group of the claims of those visitors who come to the
parks for walking.

4 David: I think the people who, er, do a lot of walking
have got more right to it than, er, you know, the
machines have, the cars and buses and things.

5 Marianne: Yeah, well we'll have to consider their point of
view as well.

As with the previous example, Marianne's reply can be seen as a
tactful move to avoid a head-on clash between members of the group
who are stressing the needs of walkers and those who are stressing
the needs of motorists. However, it is also a necessary cognitive
strategy, for the 'National Parks' topic is analogous to a committee
issue; any reasonable discussion would involve mediation between
the conflicting interests of hikers, motorists and local communi-
ties. For this purpose, Marianne is making a valuable 'chairman's
move' in explicitly acknowledging conflicting points of view.

As we have already seen in Group 4's 'Work and Energy' discussion, when Bill is compelled to answer the set question 'Is work
always done when energies change in form?' he parries this with 'No
not always. It depends what you'd classify as work.' Bill, like
other boys and girls in the groups, was having difficulty in using
the given definition of 'work' ('Work is done when a force moves')
and was finding it easier to use everyday versions of the concept.
The phrase 'It depends ...' can be interpreted in two ways. Bill
may be showing himself to be aware that he is moving between different definitions and that these must affect his reply to the
question. On the other hand the strategy may be habitual: it is
difficult to tell when an habitual phrase becomes a strategy of
thought. His physics teacher would probably not approve of his
strategy; our interest, however, lies in noticing his nascent
awareness of what he is doing.

On another occasion Bill again uses a similar method to deal with
a difference of opinion. Group 4 are talking about the social
context in which the story of 'The Pearl' is set.

61 Bill: ... around that age when everybody was sort of
primitive in that area.

62 Alan: Not so primitive really because ...

63 Bill: Well?

64 Alan: If you look at the doctor, he had, he had choco-

              late and he had guards and that, didn't he really?
              Servants.

   65 Bill: Well, primitive in the way that people didn't have
              tractors and ploughs and sort of ...

From one point of view Bill is defending himself from Alan's contrary argument, but underlying this seems to be the realisation that they are disagreeing because they are using different definitions of 'primitive'. It is an important cognitive ability to see one's own and others' knowledge as constructs which depend upon underlying assumptions, which are often unstated. Alan and Bill throughout Group 4's discussions from time to time identify differences of assumption which underlie surface clashes of opinion.

Such awareness of alternative constructions is important not for its own sake but as a step towards finding a framework in which both are meaningful. This does not mean reconciling them: the framework may supply grounds for understanding why the two viewpoints are irreconcilably different. It will be remembered that Alan contributed to the discussion of 'Steve's Letter' the idea that an appropriate style depends on the writer's relationship with the recipient: 'It depends who he's writing to really.' However, the members of the group continued to express contrary views, some wishing Steve to express violent dissatisfaction in order to satisfy his indignation, whilst others wished him to write 'respectfully', as to an older man. It was not until much later in the discussion that Group 4 began to find a framework which made sense of both these points of view, after having returned several times to this issue:

   160 Bill: You want to tell him you didn't really enjoy it
              but then again you don't want to tell him, you
              don't want to be, erm, sort of, left out in the
              cold next year so you haven't got er, a job.

Bill seems to be on the edge of grasping that the letter needs to be polite enough not to break off communication, but strong enough to make it clear that Steve would not accept the job again without better working conditions. (We found that our groups commonly returned several times to unsolved issues. Each time the issue was tacitly abandoned, but after a while it was introduced again, often with added insight gained from the intervening discussion of related matters. It seems likely that this cyclic pattern is typical of informal discussions.)

In the last two cases quoted, the acknowledgment that others' points of view are valid goes far beyond being a skilful gesture of social tact. Bill is seeking a relationship between the two viewpoints, an overarching principle which will contain both of them. This is indeed an important ability which underlies a wide range of higher-level cognitive skills.

Evaluating

It should not be thought that the groups were always concerned to achieve consensus, that they always avoided evaluating their own or others' contributions, or the overall achievement of the group. We have already looked at clashes of opinion: our concern here is those points at which evaluation is made explicit.

Under the heading 'Supportive behaviour' there were quoted
examples from Group 1 and Group 4 of their ability to encourage one
another. Bill says 'Yeah, that a, that's a good idea', to Pauline,
and David, in expressing his enjoyment of 'The Pearl' and his satisfaction at what their discussion has achieved, uses the same excla-
mation, 'Super'. These episodes were used there to illustrate the
young people's social skills, but they can also be considered as
examples of reflexivity. Part of these two groups' success in discussion seemed to lie in their ability occasionally to step outside
their own constructing of knowledge, and make that the object of
their attention. It should not however be concluded that such moves
were common even in Groups 1 and 4. For example, only on occasion
during the 'Work and Energy' discussions did one member of a group
praise another's contribution, and this occurred in Group 4. It
will be remembered that Bill constructed an ingenious series of
changes in the form of energy so as to link a steam engine to an
electric light bulb. Our attention here will be directed towards
Pauline's response to this.

29 Bill: Although you could erm, connect something to the
                steam engine so you could have heat to movement
                in the steam engine, the steam engine connected
                by pulley to a turbine, producing electricity to
                light a light bulb.
30 Jeanette: ⌈ Mm, mm, yeah, yeah
31 Pauline: ⌊ Hey, that's good is that.

Pauline's remark seems to be an immediate expression of admiration
of Bill's ingenuity, but also to mark a sudden insight into the
possibility of infinite strings of changes in the form of energy.
How far she is aware of the nature of this insight is, of course
another matter. This kind of explicit recognition of the appropriateness or ingenuity of a contribution is, however, relatively
rare in the discussions.

It is not difficult to find occasions when members of the groups
make sharply dismissive remarks about others' contributions; these
often seem to indicate an awareness that the discussion is not going
well. Some of these failures will be illustrated in a later
section, so that one brief example will here be enough. The two
girls who attempted the 'Carbon Dioxide in Water' task - Christine
and Margaret of Group 3 - found themselves immediately in disagreement. It will be remembered that they were asked to explain why
the apparatus only let air in by one tube and only let air out
through the other.

4 Margaret: Aw, well. 'Cos that'ns a long 'un, 'cos that'ns
                a long 'un and that'ns a little 'un. An' it goes
                in through't long 'un then out't little 'un. No,
                it goes in through't long 'un ...
5 Christine: You don't know what you're talking about.
6 Margaret: No, no.
7 Christine: No you see, there's a little stopper, and it's got
                two holes in.
8 Margaret: I know, I said that.
9 Christine: You didn't.
10 Margaret: No I didn't say that, but I meant that.

Christine's judgment that Margaret doesn't know what she is talking

about, though perhaps justified, takes the thinking no further. It
operates merely as a means of silencing Margaret so that Christine
can take the floor, as in fact she does at the next utterance, No.
11. (It is relevant to note that when these girls do take part in
Group 3's discussions they are frequently aggressive to one another.) In this case the negative evaluation seems to have contributed nothing to the ensuing construction of knowledge: it acts
as a dismissal of Margaret as well as her contribution. When a
qualifying move follows an inadequate contribution, it can reinforce
what is valid in what has been said, and by modifying the line of
thought, offer a profitable direction to the discussion. We have
not found in the discussions any occasions when an explicit negative
judgment seems to have helped the group towards better thinking:
expressions of alternative opinion which do not damage the group
member's self-respect seem more valuable.

Awareness of strategies

One would not expect thirteen-year-olds to plan an agenda for themselves, and few groups in fact did so. Where detailed questions
were given most groups followed these in the given order, though
Group 12 inexplicably began the 'Spaceman' task thus:

1 Nicola: Right, are we doing number four? Have we to do
              number four first?
2 Teresa: Read it out (Whispered) Read it out
3 Nicola: No, why?
4 Teresa: They know what the question is
5 Sheila: Well they'll already know
6 Nicola: Oh, yeah, well I know what. If we read the little
              introduction bit they'll know what we're on about
              about, what, we're on about.
7 Teresa: Yeah, then we can all discuss after it then.

Group 12 show themselves unusually aware of the future audience for
their recording, and are well able to plan for its needs, making
deliberate choices of the order in which they answered the
questions.
  Where no sequence of questions had been provided all groups set
off on a topic chosen at random. This proved to be an appropriate
strategy. It would only be possible to set up an agenda on the
basis of an existing sense of what issues were relevant, and which
had priority of importance; the whole purpose of topics such as
'The Pearl' and 'Gang Violence' was that through talk the groups
should shape such a sense of relevance and priority. To set up an
agenda they would need already to have partly achieved this. Although the discussion was often circular, returning to a topic
several times, there was often a perceptible improvement in the
group's grasp of the issue each time they returned. For example,
Group 4 in discussing 'Steve's Letter' returned again and again to
their disagreement about whether it should frankly express Steve's
feelings or be framed in a respectful tone.
  We have already discussed under the heading 'Social Skills' the
means by which the groups controlled their progress through the
tasks and determined the boundaries of what was relevant. Much of

this was carried out implicitly, through the give and take of
eliciting and responding moves of various kinds. Where choices were
made explicitly, this could equally have been discussed here as an
example of reflexivity. The examples used in the same section to
discuss how groups negotiate agreement upon when they have completed
their task could similarly have been used here.

One means by which a group can monitor its progress through a
discussion, and check upon points of agreement and disagreement, is
through summarising. A person who offers a summary is often for the
moment detaching himself from the give and take of the group: such
'chairman's moves' may be potentially threatening to a group's sense
of a common purpose, since the temporary chairman may seem to be
claiming authority. The presence of the tape recorder on several
occasions gave a reason for a summarising move, though as we have
seen in Group 15, Barry's 'We've now done two, Tape', is part of an
attempt to make the running which is soon challenged by the others.
Jeanette's easy summary of Bill's long description of the doctor in
'The Pearl', 'Money grabbing, you mean?' is much less threatening,
because she is clearly doing so in order to confirm that she has
understood. But this is not the kind of summary which we are referring to. What is particularly valuable is the summary which is
itself a major contribution to the constructing of knowledge, by
putting together in one statement a number of viewpoints which had
been offered separately.

A form of summarising is used occasionally to close off an
episode in preparation for moving to another topic. Most changes of
topic are carried out either implicitly in the course of a series of
expansion moves or through an initiating move which redirects the
discussion after a pause. In one or two cases, however, the
initiating move is preceded by a brief summary. Group 1, talking
about 'The Pearl', have put forward several episodes which seem to
them to lack verisimilitude, and Barbara is returning yet again to
one of these.

85 Barbara:	I think he should describe more, you know. It's supposed to be about diving and pearls.	Returning to previous sub-topic.
86 Marianne:	Yeah we don't think we don't think there's adequate description	Summarising consensus already attained.
87 David:	Yeah, no The doctor were a bit evil though wan't he?	Accepts the summary. Raises a fresh topic (related to the given task).

Marianne's summary prevented a merely repetitive return to the
earlier issues, and enabled David to move the discussion on.

In Group 3's discussion of 'National Parks' Robert summarises in
order to draw the group back on to the main issues when they appeared in danger of being sidetracked on to talk about swimming in
lakes. (Part of this exchange has already been quoted.)

23 Robert: Yeah, well the people, well most people don't like
                swimming in lakes 'cos they think they're dirty.
24 Christine: Yeah, they are.
25 Robin: More warmer anyway.
26 Robert: It's more warmer, if they build swimming pools
                it'd be warmer, more warmer, more warmer.   But
                really the National Parks were set up to, keep
                them, as natural as possible but if man keeps
                coming in and taking over all these areas, well
                there in't gonna be nowt left is there for any-
                body, any later generation?

Robert first summarises what has been said about lakes and swimming
pools, thus implicitly defining this sub-topic as completed.   Then,
signalling a change of sub-topic by the phrase 'but really', he restates the general drift of the whole discussion so far.   Then after
a pause they set out on a new sub-topic.

     In discussing reflexivity we have tried to keep in mind that the
value of reflective thought is open to question.   What we have
called 'reflexive' utterances were not very common in the discussions, and it is possible - and even probable - that there was
much more self-awareness and reflective thought than was ever put
into words.   We may indeed be mistaken in putting such emphasis upon
self-awareness: as we have shown, there was much good discussion in
the groups that organised itself without recourse to explicit self-
monitoring.   This was particularly true when members of the group
could confidently and briefly answer the set questions.   Under these
circumstances neither tentativeness nor a high level of reflexivity
seemed necessary: both are perhaps most called for when a learner
has to adapt a well-established pattern of thinking in order to cope
with new information, or with someone else's alternative pattern.
Some of the reflexive utterances illustrated here may have more
properly belonged amongst the social skills than amongst the cognitive abilities: some were certainly associated with the tactful
recognition of other people's interests.   It could be, nevertheless,
that strategies adopted in the first place in order to find social
solutions to differences of opinion may later be adapted as cognitive strategies for finding overarching principles which relate the
two.   Young people's ability to take part in social negotiation and
their ability to take account of others' viewpoints probably develop
together: it would not seem profitable to name one as cause and the
other as effect.

     Most of our examples of reflexivity have come from a relatively
limited number of boys and girls.   About a third of those quoted
came from Bill of Group 4, though the others are spread across
different groups.   It seems unlikely that this can be explained
solely in terms of intelligence; Bill's I.Q. score is somewhat
above average, but so are those of other members of these groups.
We do not want to claim more than that some members of our groups
are capable of reflexive awareness of their own and others' thinking, and that this appears to have contributed to the quality of
some of the discussions.

5   FAILURES AND LIMITATIONS

So far we have focussed on positive aspects of the children's talk,
and have attempted to instance the skills and competences which
they displayed. However, as we said earlier, the demands of the
group learning situation were complex. Inevitably, groups varied in
the success of their coping strategies; some groups which we think
of as being less successful, failed to manifest the social and
cognitive skills which we have instanced so far. In this section,
we want to describe some of the failures which occurred, since they
give some idea of the limitations of small group talk for learning
purposes. It is important to note that these less successful
strategies were relatively uncommon: overall, the children responded to the group learning situation very well. Some of these less
successful strategies are attributable to features of the task or
situation rather than to inherent failings in the children. Since
such features are open to alteration by the teacher, we shall attempt in Chapter 3 to make recommendations about ways of setting up
small group work to encourage useful talk.

Competition and conflict

We think that one of the strengths of small group work is that it
necessarily faces the learner with viewpoints different from his
own. If a learner is to achieve anything more than a simple view
of a topic it is necessary to take such other viewpoints into account, and from them to build up a more complex model. Certainly,
this is the strategy used by our more successful groups; instead
of rejecting another person's point of view as irrelevant or
'wrong', they collaboratively utilised each other's opinions, not
wholesale but with modifications, to become part of a shared understanding. This kind of synthesis, which involves admitting that
there may be something valid in the viewpoint of a person with whom
one disagrees, proved difficult for some groups. In the following
example, Glenys seems very unwilling even to hear another person's
point of view, much less consider it or concede validity to it.
These girls, from Group 11, have just begun their discussion of the
causes of 'Gang Violence' by listing the names of local gangs. When
Lesley attempts to tackle the question asked, she is very sarcasti-
cally reprimanded by Glenys.

12 Lesley:	And Stompers, Spider Boys, yes Skinheads. Well because they're bored.
13 Glenys:	You always have to get your point through don't you?

Although this is only the third time Lesley has spoken, Glenys's
accusing tone implies that Lesley has been trying to hog the conversation.

A little later Joanna repeats, albeit in different words, an
earlier point Lesley had made.

18 Joanna:	They've got nothing else to do.
19 Lesley:	They, y'know, want to show off
20 Glenys:	You've said that six times now.
21 Lesley:	Yeah you have.

22 Joanna: I know, well I'm just making my point.
23 Lesley: Yeah well you've said enough.

This effectively closes off this line of thought, for it is not
returned to. Yet other groups' exploration of the idea that facilities for entertainment for young people are lacking proved a useful
way in to the topic. What seems to happen time and time again in
Group 11's discussion is that they allow rivalry, and competition
for the floor, to stand in the way of attempts to answer the
question. Ultimately, the 'discussion' degenerates into a
'display', where the girls make competing boasts and accusations
concerning the violence of their respective boyfriends.

141 Joanna: Oh go on, you're going red, I know
142 Lesley: I'm not going red, it's Lesley that's going red
143 Joanna: Yes you are. 'My ex [i.e. 'ex-boyfriend'] used
              to be in't Green Owls'
              [Here she mimics Lesley's earlier claim.]
144 Lesley: Did he, well my ex used to be a - what did he used
              to be?
              [Lesley seems to have forgotten what she had said
              earlier and interprets Joanna as boasting about
              her own boyfriend; she therefore tries to cap the
              boast at 146.]
145 Joanna: Mine used to be a Cowboy
146 Lesley: [A Hell's Angel, that's it, then he packed it in.
147 Glenys: [They're great, Hell's Angels.

This sums up the pattern of this group's discussion; their ongoing
relationship, which is one of rivalry and aggression, continually
comes between them and the task. Any nascent attempt to turn the
conversation back to the task card's problem is cut off by the in-
trusion of moves of purely personal aggression. Thus Glenys's attempt at 60, 'Come on then, answer't question', to focus on the task
(followed by a series of short, attenuated descriptions of the
weapons used by gangs) rapidly culminates once more in the exchange
of insults:

72 Joanna: I think Lesley'd take a great Skinhead off if she
              had her hair cut.
73 Lesley: Cheeky get!

The tones of voice used throughout this discussion show that these
are not playful insults; they are exchanges of strongly-felt aggression.

    Aggression formed the pattern for another group too, though this
time the source seemed to be the difficult demands of the task
rather than existing rivalries. Group 8 working on the 'Bird's
Eggs' task had to chip a hole in the blunt end of an egg: there was
a supply of eggs, but only one saucer, and one knife, while there
were four people in the group, some of whom wanted to do the job,
some of whom did not. Those who stood by and watched acted like
back-seat drivers, to the annoyance of the one chipping at the egg:

1 Laura: Who's gonna? I'm not   Sees task as potential
            gonna do't egg   threat, and detaches
                                         herself from it.

2 Marlene: Right, chip a small hole   Claims right to give

	in the blunt end. Oh, you'll crack it all you, oh	directions to Terry who has taken the knife.
3 Terry:	This is't blunt end	Giving a reason for his action.
4 Marlene:	You silly rat you. You don't do that.	Violently accusing.
5 Terry:	Who doesn't	Rejects Marlene's right to give him orders.
6 Marlene:	You'll break't yolk	Since her claim to authority has been rejected, Marlene puts forward a rational argument by suggesting the likely outcome of Terry's actions.
7 Terry:	Well	Challenges Marlene to show that the outcome is undesirable.
8 Marlene:	You haven't to break't	Triumphantly produces the authority of the task card.

Later, when they have to crack the egg open, there is more competition over who is to carry this out. Terry fends off another attempt to interfere with:

    24 Gerroff you, I'm doing it.

This competition, accompanied by pushing, has its consequences for the state of the egg-yolk:

    31 Terry: Oh shurrup. I'll crack it into another.
    32 Laura: Break it properly.
    33 Marlene: Go on you silly rat (whispered) It's broken now with you.

The demands of this particular task seem to have been excessive. Essentially, the children had to cope with two difficult social burdens, (a) that of deciding who was to carry out necessary jobs, and (b) anxiety and uncertainty about whether they were carrying out these jobs correctly.

On once occasion this same group compete to show that they know the answers. Marlene reads aloud a question from the task card:

    60 Marlene: Will it be fertilised before the shell is put on
                  or after?
    61 Melvyn: ⌈ Before
    62 Terry: ⌊ Before
    63 Marlene: I know, I know, I'm just seeing if you knew
    64 Terry: I know alright.

Although Marlene's question at 60 looks as if she is trying to utilise the knowledge of other group members, her reply at 63 cuts

off any further elaboration. It is most unusual for pupils to ask
testing questions of this kind, though teachers ask them frequently.
Marlene is again making a tacit claim to authority, which Terry
resents.

Group 11, working on the 'Spaceman' task, provides another
example of an attempt to belittle the contributions of another
member.

66 Lesley: No, er, number three, if a piece of rock hit a
               space ship and made a hole in it ... well he'd all
               be, he'd all come out wouldn't he, for number
               three?

67 Glenys: Yeah, because
68 Joanna: We know Lesley
69 Lesley: Yeah, well I'm just checking this...

Glenys's attempt to extend Lesley's argument is sharply cut off by
Joanna. In effect, a reasonable contribution is rejected for purely
personal reasons.

To summarise, the instances so far show unresolved conflict
rather than collaboration in the task. This conflict takes the form
of competition for speech roles, competition to carry out procedures, belittlement and rejection of others' contributions, and
the exchange of insults. This competitive approach to the discussion makes these groups' attempts much less effective than those
groups whose style was more collaborative. In order to produce a
reasonable solution, they needed to utilise each other's knowledge
and resources; yet their very competitiveness prevented this from
occurring.

For another group (Group 7, working on the 'Bird's Eggs' task) it
was not competitiveness and interpersonal conflict which gave them
difficulties, but a high level of anxiety about the work they had to
do. A more extended extract than we have quoted so far gives the
flavour of this tension.

3 Bernard: That's blunt end. What do you do, cut a little
               hole in it?

4 Mary: Just cut a little hole in
5 Dorothy: No, you only do one don't you?
6 Bernard: ?
7 Mary: How you doing (whispered)
8 Bernard: Can't do it really without it breaking
9 Dorothy: Go on.
10 Mary: I've done it (whispered) Can't bleeding see.
               Ooh it's cracked. Ooh.
11 Dorothy: It's meant to be
12 Mary: Look
13 Dorothy: Oh it won't come
               (Tapping noises)
14 Mary: I've had it now (whispered)
               (Laughter)
15 Dorothy: No, I can't open it.

This concern and worry about how to carry out the manipulative
operations called for by the task card characterises most of this
group's discussion: it seems to stop them from coming to grips with
the cognitive requirements of the task. One may query why such
simple operations as chipping a hole in an egg shell, and cracking

an egg without breaking the yolk should produce such anxiety. But
when we remember that whoever was chipping or cracking the egg had
three other people, all eager to do the job, and critically watching
his or her every move, this tension becomes more understandable.
Since no one person had been assigned to do the egg-cracking, it was
open to anyone; but those watching were not passive observers:
they interfered, pushed, and made rude comments. Since the roles of
watcher and egg-cracker were frequently changed, all the group
members gradually built up a high level of anxiety. Trevor of Group
6 sums up his feelings well, after he has finished first chipping,
and then cracking the egg:

87 Trevor: You do summat. It's been murder doing this.

An unexpected feature of two groups doing the 'Bird's Eggs' task was
that they found the egg itself physically disgusting. The need to
express their distaste took precedence for a while over the task and
its questions. Indeed, on one occasion, their disgust prevented
them from looking for the nucleus in the yolk, as in the following
extract from Group 5:

20 Helen: ⌈Ugh, there's all skin hanging down, look.
              │Have you seen it? Yack!
21 Louise: ⌊Ugh, I'm not looking at that.

And again:

83 Louise: Is that it there? Hang on, I don't, I won't ugh.

Failure to challenge

Not all of the failures come from conflict or tension however. We
have mentioned the social skills developed by Group 1 in earlier
sections. From time to time, these same concerns with social
harmony lead members to fail to challenge a potentially misleading
conception, as in the following extract:

29 Marlene: Some of the other energy changes which we can use
                are, erm, hammering a nail in a wall
30 David: Yeah, 'cos erm, yeah, because the physical energy
                to grab the hammer and the hammer hits the nail
                which goes into the wall
                (Pause)

Here this group's typical style of acceptance plus elaboration leads
them not to challenge David's misleading formulation: it is not
grabbing the hammer but swinging it to the nail which is the source
of the energy. It is difficult to decide whether this represents an
inadequate grasp of the concept of energy, or merely a looseness of
phrasing.

Group 6, still on the 'Bird's Eggs' task, also fail to challenge
a very inaccurate conclusion. They have been asked to look for a
white speck on the egg's yolk, and discuss what it might be:

138 Carl: 'What do you think this is?' (Quotes task card)
139 Michelle: An eyeball
140 Ann: 'What makes you think so?' (Quotes task card)
141 Trevor: 'Crack the egg into a dish, without breaking the
                yolk. Find a small white speck on the yolk.'
                (Task card) There it is, I've got it, one white
                speck.

```
142 Carl:      It might be
143 Michelle:  It's an eye
144 Trevor:    Charming
145 Michelle:  I think anyway
```

This is an instance when some argument might have led to a more rational conclusion. Note that no justification is given for why it should be an eye.

Upon other occasions too, consensus and a smooth social surface were pursued at the expense of the cognitive demands of the task. Group 12. working on Question 2 of the 'Spaceman' task, provide an example. They have been trying to think of a reason for the cork's flying out of the bottle when the pressure outside the bottle had been lowered.

```
15 Teresa:   So that, erm, made it possible for the cork to
             come out they
16 Nicola:  ⌈Well it didn't actually come out, it were sort of
             forced out really
17 Teresa:  ⌊Yeah
18 Nicola:   And there were all pressure, all the way round it,
             all them little particles floating about
19 Teresa:   Yeah
20 Nicola:  ⌈They were forcing the cork to come out anyway
21 Teresa:  ⌊Mm
```

Teresa is providing social support, encouraging Nicola to continue talking, when she would do better to evaluate critically the content of Nicola's formulation, 'all the way round it'. They are evidently satisfied with Nicola's account, for they immediately move on to the next question, yet Nicola has missed the crucial point of the importance of the different levels of pressure inside and outside the corked bottle.

Some girls working on the 'Gang Violence' task (Group 10) provide our final example. In just fourteen utterances they conclude that gang violence is caused by boredom and lack of leisure facilities. Their style is very collaborative: they support and extend each other's contributions, manifesting the same social skills that we have praised earlier. When Tracy concludes at utterance No.16 that they have finished, no one challenges her: they are all evidently satisfied that they have answered the question adequately. Their simple view compares badly with the more complex solutions of other groups, complexities which are derived from the interchange of points of view. It seems that groups which are too preoccupied with consensus are likely to learn less from their discussion.

We have now looked at occasions where the lack of social skills hampers a group, and also where over-emphasis on collaboration inhibits learning. We now want to turn to those occasions when the cognitive strategies utilised by the children seem inadequate.

Unsuccessful cognitive strategies

For Group 9, working on the 'Gang Violence' task, the task card's questions seem to spark off reminiscences of their past experiences, but they fail to draw from these reminiscences generalisations which would be relevant to their task.

17 Shirley:	Oh is it David, you know, David tried to join a gang like that
18 Elizabeth:	And he did
19 Catherine:	Yeah I know, just because his friends did and he thought if he, if he din't
20 Elizabeth:	He'd only be't odd one out
21 Catherine:	He'd be, yeah he'd be chicken they said, and they used to pick on him. Mind you, er, Paul Jones were like that wasn't he?
22 Elizabeth:	Mm
23 Catherine:	He were, if he used to say things to us, we used to say
24 Elizabeth:	Harrison
25 Shirley:	Who's Harrison?
	(Laughter)
26 Catherine:	Oh I know, he's in jail now.

Group 9 undoubtedly have a quite detailed set of everyday experiences which are relevant to their discussion task. Examples of gang violence they know of follow on after each other like links in a chain. But these chains of first hand experience are not utilised to cast light on the question: Why do boys fight like this? The girls spend a lot of time talking, but they fail to make this talk relevant to the learning task set them.

A related strategy which limits the success of a discussion is the failure to make meanings explicit. The same group of girls on the same task provide an example of this which also includes towards the end a failure to draw relevance from what they are saying.

37 Elizabeth:	It wasn't an argument, he din't even er, anyhow, why do you think boys fight in gangs like this?... Yes, Shirley.
38 Shirley:	I wasn't saying nothing.
39 Elizabeth:	My mother says that ...
40 Catherine:	It's, it's, it's like a match in't it?
41 Shirley:	Yeah.
42 Elizabeth:	Yeah it is ...
43 Catherine:	Mind you it's impossible to change now, isn't it?
44 Shirley:	Yeah.
45 Elizabeth:	Chains
46 Catherine:	Mind you
47 Elizabeth:	Chains
48 Catherine:	If them people didn't watch the programmes that they put on, some of 'em wouldn't do it.
49 Elizabeth:	Yeah that's it they get most of the violence off the telly.

And so on at great length. What we see going on here is not the use of talk to construct new meanings but a set of unexamined platitudes which are never made quite explicit. If they had been made more explicitly, they would have been more available to criticism and modification. The girls do not advance their understanding in this extract; they merely reiterate half-understandings which they already possess.

One final example of a failure to be explicit when only explicitness will suffice comes from the girls working on the 'Carbon Dioxide in Water' task, which requires them to explain why it is

that lime water reacts differently with air which has come from the
lungs and air which has not.

20 Margaret: Erm, the air that you breathe in is erm, different
                because erm (giggles) ...
21 Christine: Go on, go on ...
22 Margaret: Don't know why it is
23 Christine: No because. Ooh we've got Mr B-- running ...
                (This refers to a teacher passing the window.)
                Erm, 'cos when you breathe, when you breathe some
                air in and then you breathe it back out again, if
                you breathe it back in again. If you breathe it
                back in again you'll die because you can't breathe
                it in. Oh I've got one of them ... I've got one
                of them. Well go on breathe in and out, no, go
                on ... (Bubbling noises) You're just breathing
                out. (Whispers and bubbling noises) And then,
                what's that last one? Oh Oh

We include this as an example of an occasion when talk does not advance understanding. What Christine says shows awareness of appropriate operations on the materials, yet she seems unable to
express her thinking explicitly enough to enable her to reflect upon
the nature of what she is doing (in spite of her use of 'if-then'
constructions). Her talk confuses herself and her partner, so that
they soon stop attempting the task.

Failure to use task card information

Another omission which seems to doom a group to failure is that of
not making connections with information and concepts from the task
card. Some groups occasionally get bogged down by very basic mis-
understandings, even though the information they need is presented
on the task card in front of them, or has been dealt with in class.
We have already mentioned how Group 4 in discussing the 'Work and
Energy' problem allow everyday conceptions of what 'work' is to re-
place the scientific definition given on the task card.

Another example comes from the girls in Group 9, working on the
'Spaceman' task. We know that two days before they came to do this
discussion, the children had been given a demonstration in class of
what happens to a corked bottle in a bell jar when the air pressure
in the bell jar is lowered. Although the task card explicitly
refers to this demonstration, the girls of Group 9 do not seem to
realise that this is what is being referred to. They recall the
contents of several previous science lessons, in an attempt to
locate one that might be relevant.

41 Elizabeth: Was it on Friday? No I didn't did I? No I wasn't
                there I don't think. Oh no I wasn't here on
                Friday was I?
42 Catherine: No it wasn't it, was ages ago was this. It really
                was.
43 Shirley: No it wasn't
44 Elizabeth: It was because do you remember, we sat together
                and (Whispering)
45 Elizabeth: I think, I don't know when it was. Erm, hang on
                let's have a look

46 Catherine: (Untranscribable)
47 Elizabeth: Was it that, was it that imploding can?
Strictly speaking, the task card contains enough information for the
girls to reason out an answer, rather than recalling one. During
their discussion, the fact that they are unsure which lesson the
task card links up with makes them panic, and they are unable to
answer the questions.

Failure to apply the task

Most of the groups went through the task in an ordered way, checking
as they went along that they had covered everything the task card
asked them to. Occasionally, a group would seem to pay little attention to the task card's question, so that their discussion, although possibly satisfying to them, could not be rated as having
produced anything like an adequate answer. We have already mentioned the implicitness and lack of relevance which characterised the
talk of Groups 9 and 10 when they worked on the 'Causes of Gang Violence' task. It is worth noting that this was accompanied by a
failure to produce an answer to the task. They do talk; some of
the talk is related to 'delinquency' or 'violence'; but they do not
actually turn this talk to the task card's specific question. This
can be contrasted with the equally unsuccessful group of girls already quoted doing the 'Carbon Dioxide in Water' task, who certainly
attempted to tackle the specific issued raised by the questions, but
whose existing knowledge was not equal to the task.
   Even groups whose skills we have quoted in earlier sections have
their limitations. Group 4, working on 'Steve's Letter', ultimately
came to a very thorough consideration of the implications of different ways of formulating Steve's basic message. But although their
overall solution is a complex one, this complexity co-exists with
some quite naive approaches.
   Just prior to the following exchange, Bill has said that he finds
the terminology of the letter off-putting, especially the references
to 'spitting' and 'fag-ends':
   19 Bill: ⎡ .... I think he could put that better
   20 Alan: ⎣ Mm ... yeah, sounds a bit disrespectful
   21 Pauline: Oh I think it's true
   22 Bill: Yeah I know it's a bit disrespectful to put that
                 down in't it?
   23 Jeanette: It's how he feels in't it?
                 (Pause)
   24 Pauline: I agree with that first bit
In this extract, we see Bill reflecting on the appropriateness of
the terms and style of the letter, which is essentially what the
task card requires. Co-existing with this is the standpoint of
Pauline and Jeanette who champion the cause of Steve, taking over
his indignation so fully that they can conceive of the letter only
as an opportunity to express this: 'It's how he feels.' They do
not manage to take into account the possibility that he might wish
to express his objections in moderate tones so as to keep open the
possibility of future employment. Their indignation against unfair
employers leads them to treat the letter as spontaneous outpouring,

and not as an object of Steve's own making that could be shaped to
more complex ends.

Uncertainty about completion of task

We have claimed above that one way in which groups failed was by not
responding to the demands of the task. Now, we look at the opposite
case: a group who cover the task card's questions over and over
again without seeming to relaise that they have already done them.
The discussion of Group 9 on the 'Spaceman' task is one of the
longest ones we recorded, yet much of it is repetition of ground already covered. Sadly their understanding does not seem to advance
with each succeeding attempt. They make nine separate attempts to
answer the first question of the 'Spaceman' task, that is to discuss
the relationship between the pressure in the bottle and the pressure
in the bell jar; eight attempts to decide why the cork came out;
only two attempts to say what would happen to the air in a spaceship
if a rock made a hole in it; and four attempts to work out what
would happen to the spaceman who stepped into space without a space
suit on. Their thinking is so confused that they do not seem to
have any 'strategy' at all, and their attempts at the different
questions are so tangled together that they themselves do not know
if they have already tried to answer a question, and if so, what
answer they came to.
    At 120, Shirley is still working on Question 3:
    120 Shirley: It will escape
    121 Elizabeth: Run away
    122 Catherine: But we've got to find out the reason why
    123 Elizabeth: Number Three
    124 Shirley: Number Two - Why did the cork ...?
    125 Elizabeth: Well, they said what would happen to the air
                   inside?
    126 Shirley: Cos there were more pressure wasn't there, in't
                   bottle?
    127 Catherine: Oh it would excape
    128 Elizabeth: It would escape
    129 Catherine: Why did the, right, number one
    130 Shirley: Why did the cork, oh.
Here they are simultaneously attempting Questions 1,2 and 3, without
realising what they are doing, or recalling that they have already
tackled each of these questions. Panic shows very strongly throughout Group 9's discussion: they interpreted the group discussion
task as a test, and behaved accordingly.
    This concludes our discussion of the limitations of group
learning. Some of these limitations and failures may have come from
the children themselves. But, as we mentioned at the beginning of
this section, many also came from features of the situation they
were in. In the next chapter we discuss some features of task and
context which tend to foster useful talk.

Chapter 3

STUDYING GROUP TALK

Many teachers use one form or other of group work, even if it is no more than a convenient device for carrying out practical work economically. Some teachers will occasionally say, 'Discuss it with your neighbour for a couple of minutes', whilst others organise formal groups which work together for weeks or months.

But whatever pattern is adopted, the teacher is bound to wonder at some point whether the children are getting all they can from the group's work. This general consideration is likely to take the form of specific queries concerning the way groups should be set up, how to structure the tasks they are to work on, and the form and style of the teacher's own participation. We cannot offer simple answers to these questions, but we can make some tentative suggestions based on our experience. However, since any recommendations we make are limited in their applicability by the relatively small number of groups we have studied, we feel that rather than applying any such recommendations wholesale, a teacher interested in the effectiveness of his class's group work should record some of this talk for his own study. From critical listening, alone or with colleagues, teachers can come to understand better what goes on in small group discussion and how they can best contribute to it. We hope that our own work will provide a framework of information and alternatives on which teachers might draw in the creation of their own insights.

In order to try out any of our suggestions, a teacher would need to have access to a tape recorder, and be able to use it. Much may be learned from even one or two recordings of children working in small groups, so a teacher whose school does not have one, and who does not own one himself, could perhaps borrow one from a friend on one or two occasions and still gain valuable insights, although we believe that greater spin-off will be gained from having a variety of group discussions to contrast with one another.

1 ATTITUDES TO PUPILS' CONTRIBUTIONS

A most important influence on how the pupils approach tasks in small groups is likely to be the way in which teachers normally treat their contributions in lessons, though no direct evidence of this

came from our study. The children whom we came to know well, and
who worked with us frequently (Groups 1-4) were more successful in
making sense of the given tasks than were those others from the same
school (Groups 9-16) whom we recorded all on one day without having
met them before. | We conclude from this that the children's re-
lationship with the adult who sets up small group work, be he
teacher or researcher, affects their performance in the group. In
the former case not only had we taken care to get to know the
children, but the teacher had carefully explained to them that we
were interested in finding out how they talked, and not in testing
their speech skills as if in an examination. In general we may surmise that if a teacher shows in his reception of pupils' contributions that he takes them seriously enough to reply to them, they
are more likely to take themselves seriously in attempting the
tasks. That is, the teacher's behaviour in lessons helps to determine whether pupils see themselves as capable of shaping understanding for themselves.

The very use of small group discussion in lessons is a powerful
way of showing that the teacher believes in the value of talk in
learning, so that we might expect children who are used to working
together to do so with less conflict and with more ability to cope
with the social and cognitive demands of group discussions. This
happened with our groups. The children from one school, who had had
little or no experience of small group work before our project
began, had far more difficulty in sorting out who should do what,
and spent much of their time in competing for speech roles.

We were recording the pupils for research purposes, but it does
seem likely that tape recording in itself has considerable effect
on how children view their own talk. In the first place, a recording makes new opportunities for becoming aware of how we think
aloud, and this may increase the value of small group discussion by
enabling pupils to listen to and reflect upon their own strategies.
Furthermore, in our recordings, control over the tape recorder was
another means by which we could show the children that we trusted
them to take greater responsibility for their own learning by encouraging them to switch the tape recorder off, and play back
sections to themselves at will.

Listening with children to recordings of their previous discussions is also a valuable way of convincing them that their talk
is taken seriously, but it carries dangers with it. When we played
back tapes of the discussions to the children whom we had recorded
we found that some of the girls in particular were pre-occupied with
the 'unfinished' character of their talk, with the ums and ahs, the
silences and the ungrammatical sentences which changed direction in
the middle. When listening to tapes with children, it would be
useful to point out that such features are typical of talk, which is
in its nature different from writing. We realised that the children
assumed that school work had to be completed and polished, and had
not grasped that using speech in the process of shaping meaning is
also part of school learning. Perhaps teachers should help their
pupils to understand this. It was in the course of discussion about
discussion that we were able to communicate explicitly to the
children our positive feelings about their talk.

2   PUPILS' GRASP OF THE SUBJECT-MATTER

Nobody likes to be wrong, especially in front of rivals or superi-
ors, so the pupils' sense of competence, their sense of having
something relevant to contribute, will go far to determine the
morale with which they approach the task, and the patience with
which they continue to work together at it.

We had no doubt that the preliminary presentation of topics in
lessons played a considerable part in the success of some of the
groups' discussions. This does not mean that all the problems had
already been solved for them, but that the class discussion had displayed to them some of the approaches which they might use, and
shown that some of their suggestions were taken seriously by the
teacher. While the problem was being presented and some suggestions
aired, the discussions were also demonstrating that the problem
could be solved by rational means; this should make it clear to the
pupils that they are expected to think and not merely to remember,
as did Group 9 in their despairing attempts at the 'Spaceman' task.

In many cases groups had materials before them to which they
could turn for help. Sometimes these were printed documents, and
sometimes apparatus. In lessons pupils turn to the teacher for
authoritative help; by withdrawing, the teacher throws responsibility back upon the pupils, who therefore tend to make use of any
available resources, both those in their own memories and those on
the desk before them. If children have access to apparatus, this
often improves the quality of the discussion above the standard obtained if they are required to talk about something presented to
them completely abstractly. In science and some humanities tasks,
it may be easy for the teacher to build manipulation of materials
into most tasks: and it seems that for groups working on literary
tasks, the actual poem or prose extract serves the same purpose as,
say, observable apparatus.

The subject matter of some tasks set to children may be familiar
to them already. This familiarity may derive from the fact that the
material has already been covered thoroughly in class, or it might
be that it connects well with the children's experiences in the
everyday world. We have already discussed some examples of each of
these cases. In the 'Spaceman' task, the preparatory work in class
helped all except one of the groups (Group 9, girls) to interpret
the demands of the task in a way that was consonant with the
teacher's intentions. In Chapter 2, under the heading 'Constructing
the Question' we demonstrated the effort which groups put into
clarifying the issues that are involved in the task set to them.
Initial exploration of such issues in class with the teacher can
probably help groups to gain insight into the conceptual framework
within which the teacher intends their discussion to move.

On the other hand, since material that is over-familiar may not
provide the stimulus to re-shape and re-order existing constructs,
teachers may also wish to use the small group for work which is
relatively new and strange to the children. It is not necessarily
fruitful, however, to consider the effects of familiarity with the
task's content in separation from the characteristics of individual
groups. The two very similar tasks of 'Causes of Vandalism' and
'Causes of Gang Violence' would seem to draw on areas of immediate

experience and themes that would be familiar to urban thirteen-year-olds. Earlier, however, we discussed two very different styles of solution to this task. Group 1 collaborated in a productive discussion in which they built up a complex model of the kinds of social and environmental influences which may contribute to involvement in gang warfare. Group 9, equally well provided with everyday knowledge and experiences relevant to the task, failed to make explicit, to qualify, to extend or to elaborate each other's contributions in the way that helped to shape Group 1's success. (The two extracts referred to have been discussed in Chapter 2, in the sections headed 'Collaborating or defending' and 'Unsuccessful cognitive strategies' respectively.) Thus, whilst this discussion of strangeness-familiarity is one that we would suggest a teacher should be conscious of, it is unlikely to be uniquely responsible for the way children perform on a task. Rather, it seems likely that it will interact with other characteristics of the group: how well they get on together, the style they have developed, and so on.

3   HOW THE TASK IS PRESENTED

The nature and value of a discussion will be influenced not only by the content of the task, but also by the tightness or looseness with which the directions are framed. There will be some occasions when a teacher has a clear idea of the sequence of thought that he wants the group to follow, and he will therefore guide them through this sequence with a 'tight' series of questions. On other occasions a teacher will not wish to predetermine the route which is to be followed or the goal that is to be reached, though he may have clear ideas about what constitutes appropriate evidence, and perhaps about what is an appropriate strategy for coming to conclusions.

The point can be made more precisely by examining examples of 'tight' and 'loose' tasks from our materials. The 'Spaceman' task began with this preamble:
We placed a corked bottle under a bell jar. We pumped the air out of the bell jar with a vacuum pump.
Then the cork came out.
The discussion was structured first by two questions which required the children to recapitulate the principles arrived at during the preceding lesson.
1   Discuss among yourselves the relationship between the pressure in the BOTTLE with the pressure under the BELL JAR when all the air had been sucked out.
2   Why did the cork come out?
It should have been clear to the pupils from the first of these that they were expected to provide an explanation based upon the difference between the pressure in the bottle and the pressure in the bell jar: this part of the task was framed in such a way as to offer tight constraints for their answers. The other two questions follow:
3   If a piece of rock hit a spaceship and made a hole in it, what would happen to the air inside?
4   What would happen to the spaceman if he stepped out into space without a space suit on?

These seem somewhat less tight: they define particular situations
tightly for the pupils to explain, but do not make it so clear that
differential pressure is again to be used as the basis for the
explanation.

Compare this with the far looser task based on Steinbeck's story
'The Pearl':

> In the Introduction to 'The Pearl', John Steinbeck says that the
> story may be a parable and that, 'perhaps everyone takes his own
> meaning from it'.
> Discuss among yourselves what you have found in the story so
> far - the 'good and bad things, and black and white things and
> good and evil things', as Steinbeck says; and any points about
> the characters, the setting, the way the book is written, that
> you feel worth discussing.

In spite of the length of these instructions they offer little con-
straint, explicit or implicit, to the replies. Moral issues from
the story are to be discussed, but characters, setting and style are
also relevant. Moreover, 'everyone takes his own meaning from it'
is an invitation to the pupils to regard their own sense of relevance as paramount. One could not have a much looser task than
this.

If a teacher wishes his pupils to engage in exploratory talk of
this kind, it is important to indicate this in the phrasing of the
task. This is a matter of inviting a range of suggestions which the
children themselves can evaluate; this emphasises the process of
discussion rather than the conclusions reached. Since schools tend
to emphasise 'right answers', children need encouragement to feel
their way through difficult ideas, and to explore half-formed intuitions. The reader will remember from Chapter 2 Group 1's discussion of 'The Pearl' which achieved an expression of shared enjoyment that no teacher could have planned for. This group's
success perhaps reflects not only the open task but also the value
placed on exploratory talk by their English teacher. The explicitness often demanded of children in their written work, polished and
revised for presentation, implicitly devalues the exploration of
half-understood ideas, yet it is these latter which represent the
growth-points for further understanding.

It is not our intention here to imply a simple preference for
tasks which have no more than a 'loose structure'. Even adults find
an agenda a useful aid in guiding the progress of a discussion. It
can be argued that a tight series of questions performs this same
function for a group of learners. The difficulty is that in writing
the questions it is all too easy to make inappropriate assumptions
about the pupils' knowledge and insight, and their ability to apply
this to the matter in hand. The teacher may have in mind a clear
logical progress from given information to required conclusions, but
the learners may need to go by a far more roundabout route to reach
their destination, using information and experience that to the
teacher seems peripheral. Thus the best series of questions is one
which helps the learners to structure their discussion without pre-
determining its content.

The teacher must decide when it is that his pupils have enough
grasp of the subject matter to shape their own implicit agenda, and
when they need the support of a fairly tight sequence of questions.

In our materials it seemed that teachers chose to set loose tasks
when their pupils had much everyday knowledge that was relevant, as
in 'The Pearl' and in social studies topics such as 'Gang Violence'.
They tended to set tighter topics in science, where the explanations
they wanted were more removed from everyday ways of looking at
things. However it is perfectly possible for the reverse to be true
of science and social studies topics.

There are considerable dangers however, in setting up too tight a
series of directions. For example, in the 'Bird's Eggs' task the
initial instructions called for action and observation:

2 Crack the egg into a dish, without breaking the yolk.
   Find a small white speck on the yolk.
   What do you think this is?

This question was not, however, open to discussion solely on the
basis of observation and the common-sense knowledge available to the
children. Several of the groups did not find it easy to change
their strategy from descriptive observation to the generating of a
sequence of possible explanations of the white spot. (It is possible that here we have a clash between what the children thought of
as normal learning strategies in school and the demands of this
task.)

Terminology too can create problems. One group of girls found
confusing the phrase 'under the bell jar' in the preamble to the
'Spaceman' task. They saw the bottle as being IN the bell jar, and
were held up while they puzzled at the conventional formulation.
(A moment's consideration of the shape and use of a bell jar will
explain the nature of the confusion: the bottle was 'under' to the
teacher who placed the bell jar on top of it, perhaps.)

After our work with these groups we concluded that there is much
to be said for ending even the tightest task with an open invitation
to discuss other related issues which occur to pupils. Even the
most experienced teacher cannot predict all the problems that face
each group of his pupils in understanding the topic under discussion; he may have the responsibility for making available to
pupils traditional ways of solving problems in that subject, but he
should not forget their private problems of understanding which they
may need to sort out first. We have found that some pupils see
valuable and relevant possibilities in manipulating apparatus. At
times this is no more than a matter of strengthening their intuitive
grasp of the physical principles involved, but in one or two cases
we have found particular groups able to use apparatus for trying out
new hypotheses of their own. Any such signs of ability to carry out
independent learning are, we believe, worthy of encouragement.

When teachers set up group work it is often because they place
more emphasis upon the journey than upon the destination, because
they are more interested in developing their pupils' ability to
think than in taking them to specific conclusions. We have already
suggested that it may be useful to frame questions in ways which ask
pupils to provide not one explanation, but several alternative
explanations, and to encourage them to consider what arguments can
be put forward in support of each of them. Moreover, when a teacher
joins in a group's discussion the kinds of questions he asks will
implicitly inform his pupils whether he is more interested in right
answers or in the strategies by which valid answers may be arrived
at.

It is also relevant to consider the likely effect of asking the children to write about what they have been discussing. From one point of view this seems an admirable device for encouraging them to clarify and make explicit to themselves what understandings they have achieved during discussion. On the other hand, if they perceive the writing as an assessment of their achievement it may cause them to avoid exploratory strategies and pursue right answers. In some cases, as with our Group 9, it may cause such anxiety that they abandon rational strategies and fall back upon mechanical recollections, appropriate or not. The girls of Group 9, since they knew they must write without one another's support, concentrated their efforts on memorising such bits of knowledge as they could put together, going over these repeatedly without advancing their understanding. Thus the setting of written work can reflect back different constraints on the discussion which precedes it, according to how the pupils perceive the purposes of that writing.

We have suggested so far that both tight and loose tasks have their uses as stimuli for learning talk. We have indicated both the way in which the structure of a tightly-knit task can lead groups to the teacher's goal, as well as the possibilities for exploration offered by tasks which do not lay down specific agendas. We also claimed much earlier in our discussion, that the successful management of the cognitive demands of the task along with the social demands of the discussion situation, was a considerable challenge to children of this age. It seems reasonable therefore to build into the instructions to the group some suggestions for ways of coping with these demands, suggestions which do not stop groups from exploring their own lines of thought, but rather help them to do so more systematically. One way of helping groups to work systematically might be to appoint one or more children to 'chairman'-like roles. But in our experience children of this age do not find it easy to chair a group tactfully, nor to accept the guidance of a chairman of their own age. Rather we suggest that by building special directions into the task card, responsibility for 'chairman'-like functions may be shared equally among all group members. We offer an example of such a device below, which might prove useful with older children. It is intended only as a suggestion that could be revised to suit different situations. Its aims are to help the children be more aware of what they are doing, and of how they are using the talk; and also to help them evaluate the discussion so far in terms of its relevance to their purposes, and the quality of the argument. In this example, some writing is incorporated at the end of the discussion, but this writing is meant to be a private summary of the individual's own understandings, in note form, rather than a polished account to be read by others.

1 After you've been talking for about five minutes ask yourselves: 'How far have we got? Are we on the point or have we been sidetracked? What line should we follow up next?' (Don't spend more than about two minutes on this, though.)
2 At the end of the talk allow yourselves several minutes to decide together what have been the main points of your discussion and the arguments that have been put forward.
3 Write down in note form a brief summary of the discussion. Keep these notes for yourself as a record of what was said.

You will probably find them useful to refer to for future work.

4   THE COMPOSITION OF THE GROUPS

In considering those discussions which seemed least successful, we identified two contrasting styles of approach, as we described in Chapter 2. At the one extreme, some groups seemed unable to cope with clashes of opinion without these turning into personal disputes which might degenerate into aggression and insults. At the other extreme, some groups seemed so eager to preserve an unruffled surface of consensus that they avoided any expression whatsoever of contrary opinions. This meant that obvious mistakes were allowed to go unchallenged. Such groups used their social skills at the expense of their cognitive strategies. This strategy arises mainly from fear, and is likely to disappear whenever a group feels that its contributions are worthwhile and valued by others.

We suggest two, three or four members as the optimum size of discussion or work groups for children around the 11-15 age group. Two is clearly the minimum number for a dialogue to take place: and to have more than four children to a group often results in one or more members remaining silent, rather than participating. Clearly, where the time available for the discussion is itself limited, the addition of an extra person to the group means less time available for each group member to talk. But apart from this consideration, we also believe that to have a fifth or sixth member imposes strains on the social organisation of the group which diverts the children from their main task. The basic task of ordering the discourse - who talks, and when - becomes too difficult for children who are used to being controlled by the teacher.

This is especially evident where the group is required to manipulate a shared set of apparatus, as we have seen. The larger the group, the harder it is to decide who shall be the one to carry out the actual manipulations of the apparatus, and inevitably, some members cannot get close enough to the apparatus to observe it properly, and thus get really involved in what is going on.

For many children in their early teens, it seems that single-sex groups are slightly more comfortable, and less challenging. Given the choice, most groups would end up as single-sex ones (we are obviously talking about co-ed schools where the choice is meaningful), because children at this age seem to define as 'friends' members of their own sex only. Where the teacher arbitrarily 'mixes' the groups, then some of the group's task inevitably becomes that of coping with working in this unaccustomed situation. The two sex groups may even polarise, into 'girls versus boys', and the discussion may become competitive rather than co-operative. But what effects may this have on the learning that takes place in the groups?

We suggest that this depends on how accustomed the members are to the experience of working in small groups. Everyday experience tells us that we talk most openly with people we know well, and whom we trust. In this situation, our talk is oriented to 'sharing' our experiences and ideas whereas with people we don't know so well, or

trust, we are obliged to 'present' to them a public face. (1) But
'sharing', although valuable, in its very nature may not provide the
impetus to push our understandings to their limits, and to make them
explicit as we must when talking with people who don't share our
world view. We can get by with vague, imprecise formulations talking with friends, that would be challenged by others. But we
believe that it is this challenge to make explicit and to redefine
that plays an important part in learning.

Our solution is to suggest that decisions about the sex composition of the groups, and therefore about whether they are
friendship or arbitrary groups, should derive from a consideration
of how familiar the children in question are with the experience of
working in small groups and how well they grasp the material that
constitutes the task.

If they have not done much recording, or small group work,
before, it is probably best to make the groups single-sex, self-
selected groups, to minimise the social problems that have to be
dealt with in addition to the set task. But later on, as they
become more skilled at coping with the small group situation (and
used to the tape recorder), then it can be useful to mix the groups
for sex and to select members arbitrarily.

When a class is not used to group work there is much to be said
for allowing the children to choose friends to work with, and for
seeing to it that each group task arises out of the shared classwork
and feeds back quickly into it. Once pupils are accustomed to working in this way they will be able to sustain longer periods of independent group work, and to cope with the social problems of collaborating with classmates with whom they are not on close terms.

Similarly, where groups are making an initial exploration of
difficult material, it would be wiser to allow the children to
explore their half-intuited knowledge tentatively, and to reformu-
late as they go along. But where the material is not so difficult,
or where the children have got byond the initial, exploratory stage
and the teacher wishes them to tighten up their argument, and justify their thinking, then the mixed group will be more appropriate, as
it is here that arguments are more likely to be challenged, and
justification required by group members holding opposite views.

5 EQUIPMENT

The teacher may have little control over the kind of recording
equipment he uses, having to make do with whatever is available.
Where choice between a conventional tape recorder and a cassette
recorder is possible, we should point out that cassettes have the
advantage of being light-weight and easily portable. However, their
big disadvantage for this kind of work is that it is difficult to
pinpoint a particular place on a cassette recorder, as may sometimes
be necessary when working on analysis of the tapes. With conventional tape recorders, on the other hand, it is very easy to
locate specific sections using the revolution counter. Good quality
recording equipment is very expensive, but not really necessary for
the limited purpose of playing one's tapes back to a few people in
a small room.

It is important to remember that many microphones are direction-
al, that is, they pick up best sounds that are coming from a specified direction. Sounds from other sources will be muffled or in-
audible, so it is obviously necessary to position children appropriately for the microphone in question. Generally, the quality of
sound is improved if the microphone is placed on some soft material,
such as a rolled-up coat, which will absorb some of the vibrations
from the floor. Touching or tapping the microphone produces loud
and unpleasant noises on the tape, so it is best to ask the children
not to touch it.

If at all possible, it will be well worth carrying out the
recording in a separate room, away from where the rest of the class
is working. This may pose problems of supervision, but the added
clarity of the recording makes the attempt worthwhile. Microphones
are as sensitive as ears but less selective. They pick up everything within their range, relevant or irrelevant, whereas ears
filter out unimportant noise. In a busy school (especially one with
hard floors), this can mean that extraneous sounds are recorded,
such as footsteps, desks and chairs scraping, other voices, etc.,
and these noises may make it impossible to hear the discussion
itself. If groups must be recorded in the classroom, with other
activities going on in the background, it is best to have someone
holding the microphone close to whoever is speaking. Wherever the
recording is done, it is feasible to make older children responsible
for some aspects of the recording. We feel that this makes the
recording a matter of collaboration rather than something which is
imposed upon them. It is possible that the children may think the
recording is an ill-disguised test, and this is an impression to be
avoided if one wishes the children to be natural and relaxed.

6   RECORDER SHYNESS

We feel that it is unreasonable to combine the experience of being
tape recorded for the first time with that of working in groups for
the first time. We therefore prefer only to record children who are
fairly used to working in small groups. Otherwise, the combined
pressures of coping with a new and unfamiliar social situation at
the same time as coping with feelings of microphone shyness may
prevent the children from making the best use of the learning situation. Where children are already accustomed to small group work,
we have been surprised at the assurance they have shown. However,
we do follow a fairly standardised procedure which is aimed at
reducing microphone shyness.

Before leaving the groups alone to start their first recorded
task, we record a small amount of talk. This may consist of a
demonstration of how to use the tape recorder, presenting the
children with the task card, and talking about what the children are
meant to do. If the researcher or teacher talks naturally whilst
the recorder is on, the children are less likely to feel shy.
Usually, enough questions are asked by the children during this procedure to ensure that each one has said something spontaneously.
Anyone who doesn't talk may perhaps be gently persuaded to say
something short and neutral, even if it is only to read out the
title of the task card.

Children who have not heard their recorded voices before are
usually curious to hear what they sound like, but they may be disappointed to hear something that sounds unfamiliar. The sound of
one's voice heard as one talks is of course often quite different
from the way it sounds to other people, or when played back on tape.
As we play back the preliminary section of tape, therefore, we try
to allow time for the expression of embarrassment or complaints. We
point out that most people find the sound of their own recorded
voice strange the first time they hear it. Additionally, we briefly
explain to the children why their voices sound so different on the
tape: we explain that since the tape picks up only a certain pro-
portion of their voices' characteristics, and distorts them slightly, their voices don't necessarily sound to other people (or to
themselves) the way they sound as transmitted from the tape
recorder. This initial procedure and explanation need only take a
few minutes, and of course, need only be carried out the first time
the children record.

However, we would suggest that whenever possible the children
should be allowed to play back part of their discussion. The
children almost always ask for this, or accept it with pleasure if
it is offered, and it seems a small enough repayment for their
efforts. Usually, they want to listen just for curiosity's sake,
but we have argued above that for the teacher to listen to the tape
of some group work with the children involved can have some very
valuable results.

One final suggestion for reducing microphone shyness is that the
children should be shown how to stop and restart the tape recorder.
If they can stop the recorder themselves when they have finished the
task, the teacher doesn't need to be present, or within earshot,
while they are working.

7   WHY LISTEN TO GROUP TALK?

Given that a teacher already uses small group work as part of his
everyday teaching, then monitoring the performance of some of these
groups can enhance his understanding of the way they work. He can
gain insights that will enable him to make future discussions more
effective in terms of the learning that goes on in them. These
insights can be grouped into the following areas:

1   By listening to recordings a teacher can check whether
    children have fully comprehended material presented to them in
    class, and whether they have grasped essential principles and
    can apply them. Recording the children has the obvious ad-
    vantage that it constitutes a permanent record of what the
    children said, so the teacher may stop it, play it back, check
    and re-check what he is hearing. The moment by moment demands
    of teaching leave no time to consider carefully what the
    children are saying so that impressions gained in class about
    the nature of the children's understanding are only too liable
    to be forgotten.
2   It may at times be more important, however, to understand HOW
    one's pupils are thinking than WHAT they are thinking. The

route by which children reach their conclusions is often very
different from that taken by the teacher. They make links
with unexpected areas of knowledge, as when Group 15 tried to
explain flat fish in terms of pressure, thus showing that they
saw pressure as exerted downwards only. They may use unexpected strategies: in setting the 'Steve's Letter' task we
expected a discussion of appropriate styles, but the children
chose to fill in hypothetical situations ('He might be an old
man, a friend like ...') as if the context we had given was
too thin to make a judgment possible. Thus there is value in
understanding how children arrive at their conclusions which
is quite separate from deciding whether the conclusions themselves are acceptable.

3   Information can also be gained about the suitability of tasks
and materials to the children. The concepts may be too difficult or too obvious; the pupils may need new information or
more experience with other examples; the questions may be
ambiguous, or need to be directed more tightly or more loosely. In general, listening to children who are using a work-
sheet suggests how it might be revised before it is used
again.

4   The teacher can monitor the social characteristics of his
successful discussion groups, so as to improve future ones.
We have discussed single-sex versus mixed groups, and the
influence upon the group's talk of members' familiarity with
each other, but we have not been able to give any conclusive
recommendations that would hold for all children. Listening
in on the groups helps the teacher to work out the most appropriate and helpful way of setting up groups from his
particular class.

5   Another spin-off from listening to pupils' discussions is that
they often show skills in the discussion groups that go un-
noticed, or are not called for, in the full class. In our experience, teachers have gained new insights into their pupils'
strengths as well as their weaknesses by listening to group
talk.

6   The final reason we can suggest for a teacher to monitor
pupils' discussion groups is to gain insights on the effect of
his own participation in those groups. A common way of using
small group work within the lesson framework is for the
teacher to present material to the full class, then to ask the
class to perform some operations on this material while working in small groups, and then for the teacher to move around
the class from group to group, questioning, encouraging, ex-
postulating. But what does his intervention do? He may feel
the need to modify the way he participates in these groups
when he has had the opportunity to listen to and reconsider
his teaching strategies.

8   LISTENING TO THE RECORDINGS

We do not recommend that teachers attempt to make written transcriptions of discussions as a whole. For research purposes it can

be essential to make detailed and highly accurate transcriptions, which identify all speakers, indicate the length of pauses, and include false starts, 'ums' and 'aahs' and so on. This would be very time-consuming, however, and also inappropriate to most teachers' purposes. The focus of interest for the teacher will be on the quality of the learning that has gone on, and the role played in this learning by talk. These can be judged without making full transcriptions.

The approach we suggest is one whose aim is to identify those sections of the dialogue which seem to be significant for the learning process. We suggest in the first place that the teacher listen several times to the tape as a whole. In our experience, each time of listening produces new understandings and perceptions of events which were overlooked before. Even more fruitful than listening to the tapes alone would be to set up an informal working group with a small number of other teachers with similar interests. Two or three listeners are likely to produce a greater number of comments on the tape than is one alone, and in the discussion of these comments, a more complex understanding will be reached than if one has access only to a single interpretation of what is going on in the discussion.

What happens during repeated listenings is that gradually the listener constructs an understanding or an account of the progress of the talk. Once the listeners feel they have made sense of what is going on as a whole, we recommend that they then use informal discussion to choose sections from the talk which seem to be particularly interesting from the standpoint of learning. These may be short snatches only, which are judged to be particularly significant, or they may be slightly longer sections of interrelated dialogue which seem to form identifiable episodes.

These sections which are judged to be of particular significance for learning are worth discussing in detail. Their locations on the tape should be taken down (by reference to the revolution counter) so that they can be gone over and considered repeatedly. If anyone in the teachers' group has time, it will be useful to transcribe these sections, since it is easier to work on transcripts than on tapes alone. If no one has time to transcribe even these excerpts, then much can be learned from repeated listenings and discussion with others, coupled with a synopsis in note form of the main points that arise in the discussion, so that these can be referred to later.

This practical advice, however, does not approach the problem of what one looks for when listening to recordings. We cannot tell teachers what to look at: that depends on what they want to know. Researchers have developed category systems for analysing lessons or small group discussions, but these systems may conceal what teachers want to know instead of making it clear. It is sometimes difficult when faced with a new recording of group talk to decide where to begin to discuss it. The following questions provide no more than starting-points.

1   What are the children doing in their talk? What are they 'using talk for'? This is often a useful starting point since it can lead to discussion both of the content of what is said and of the social processes going on.

2 What signs are there of learning going on? This can be approached either through the characteristics of the speech -
   such as hesitations and reformulations - or by analysing the
   sequence of thought. It also raises questions about what is
   meant by 'learning', and this can often be usefully discussed
   in relation to a particular conversation.

3 Talk is sometimes used for 'presenting' ideas that are already
   well-formed, and at other times for 'exploring' and shaping
   thought in new ways, that is to the speaker. Where do your
   discussions lie on the 'presenting-exploring' dimension? How
   do you know?

4 Are the pupils working together in constructing lines of
   thought? The Cognitive Strategies which we discussed in
   Chapter 2 could be used as a basis for looking at their thinking. How explicit do they make their viewpoints, especially
   when they differ from one another? Does this seem to matter?

5 What devices do the children use to organise their social relationships with one another? Which of the Social Skills
   illustrated in Chapter 2 do they display?

6 What seems to influence the relative success or failure of
   these discussions in promoting useful learning? What part in
   this is played by the subject matter and its relationship to
   what the children already know? What part is played by apparatus, pictures, objects, maps, texts, etc.? Did the way in
   which the task was set prove helpful? Might the talk have
   been better if the children had been differently grouped?

So far we have considered the children working alone, but most
teachers go round from group to group in order to join for a while
in the pupils' discussions. This may be in order to encourage the
pupils to order and clarify their thoughts by putting them into
words. The teacher may also want to direct attention to aspects of
the matter which the pupils have missed, or to head them in new directions, or to encourage them to be more self-critical. He may
want them to make practical decisions about managing materials or
apparatus, or about carrying out a longer-term piece of work. He
may wish to give them advice or information that has become necessary at that stage of the work. To carry out these purposes he will
need to listen to what the children say in order to understand where
they have reached and what their problems are, and he will have to
make his own contributions judiciously and in a form which they can
make use of. So far we have been describing ways of understanding
how pupils are thinking; we now wish to turn to ways of monitoring
the teaching that goes on when the teacher joins the group. This
will be a matter of checking that the help which he offers to his
pupils is really what he intends.

Here are some questions which teachers might use as a framework
to guide their listening to recordings of group discussions which
they have taken part in. They are necessarily general, since they
are meant to apply to a wide range of subject-matter and approaches.

1 Where did the information, new ideas and suggestions come
   from? Were they mainly from you or from your pupils? Is
   this what you wanted?

2   Does what you say seem to match with where they have got to?
    Do they understand it? Are they able to use the lead you have
    given them? Are you sure that you understood what they were
    trying to say? Did they seem to find your help useful?
3   How did you receive your pupils' reports on what they had
    done, or their suggestions for alternative possibilities? Did
    you evaluate it (explicitly or implicitly) as good or bad,
    relevant or irrelevant, true or false? If you did evaluate,
    were your responses mainly positive or negative? Or did you
    pass over unacceptable contributions in silence? What do you
    think is the best policy?
4   If you did not evaluate (or ignore) their contributions, what
    did you do with them? Did you use them as a basis for a new
    line of thought? Did you expand them yourself, or ask the
    children themselves to expand them? Did you argue back, or
    put another point of view, or ask questions directing their
    attention to snags? Did you introduce new materials or infor-
    mation? Did you encourage the pupils to devise some ways of
    finding out answers to questions? In retrospect, which of
    these things would have been most appropriate at that particu-
    lar moment?
5   Were you able to encourage the children to be more explicit
    and clear than when they were alone? Did they talk at length,
    explaining where they had got to or did they just give short
    answers and wait to see whether you approved? Were you able
    to wait for answers even when there was a long pause, or did
    you feel that the other groups needed you too much for a long
    stay with any one of them? Who summarised where the dis-
    cussion had reached? Did you in the end have to tell them the
    right answer? (Was there a right answer?)

These two sets of questions – the one for groups without a teacher
and the other for considering teaching strategies – are too general
to take the discussion far. Listening to a recording usually generates a set of questions appropriate to that recorded material,
especially when several teachers are collaborating. (2) It is
useful to ask any member of a group who makes a general statement,
such as, 'They don't seem really to be listening to one another', to
point out to the others the exact sequence of utterances that he has
in mind. This enables the others to join in direct discussion of
the evidence on which the interpretation is based.

   Our purpose in writing about these sixteen groups of adolescents
'making sense together' has been to preserve for others our insights
into the abilities and skills which they showed. We have no doubt
that when children take a major part in the control of their own
learning this often allows for the exercise of abilities which are
not evident at other times. When this is true, and under what
circumstances, is no doubt a matter for inquiry and debate. We do
not wish to argue that small group work is ideal for all children
upon all occasions, but that in general learners benefit from exercising control over what they learn and how they set about learning
it. In this last section we have discussed ways of helping pupils
to make the best of group work, and have urged teachers to find
means of monitoring group discussions. It is always valuable to

understand one's pupils better, and to see their strengths and weaknesses; many teachers are surprised by the unforeseen competences
shown in their pupils' talk. In urging teachers to listen to their
pupils learning and to themselves teaching, we are looking towards
what has been called an 'extended professionalism' (3) in teachers,
looking towards a time when teachers take it for granted that they
should assume a deliberately reflective stance towards what goes on
in their classrooms.

9 PRACTICAL NOTES

To study small group discussions you would have to bear the following points in mind:

1   The influence of your own attitudes to pupil talk: how can
    you communicate to the pupils that you think their talk is
    worthwhile?
2   Pupils' grasp of the subject matter:
    (i)   Content of the task - familiar or strange? Will pupils
          be using everyday knowledge or new conceptual
          structures?
    (ii) Written or pictorial or filmed material?
    (iii) Apparatus to be manipulated?
3   How the task is presented:
    (i)   'Tight' or 'loose' structure?
    (ii) Emphasis on getting to a 'correct' answer or on the
          quality of the discussion?
    (iii) Must a solution be agreed on and presented in writing?
          Can there be only one solution?
    (iv) Is descriptive observation and action called for, or
          the generation of rationally argued explanations?
    (v)   Whether to use an agenda, or to instruct the children
          to recap and summarise and to share chairman-like
          functions?
    (vi) Invitation to discuss new but related issues?
4   Composition of the groups:
    (i)   Size and sex of group?
    (ii) Should members choose one another?
5   Equipment:
    (i)   Tape or cassette?
    (ii) Trying to ensure good quality sound
    (iii) Recording in separate room?
6   How to minimise recorder shyness:
    (i)   Allowing children time to get used to their own record-
          ed voices
    (ii) Teacher making sure his/her own voice is recorded too
    (iii) Encouraging expression of children's reaction to the
          sound of their own voices
    (iv) Giving children some control over the tape recorder
    (v)   Allowing them to replay their own discussion
7   Listening to the recordings:
    (i)   Alone or with an informal working group?
    (ii) Repeated listening - sorting out what is happening

   (iii)   Decisions about what you are looking for:
- a talk that is significant for learning
- b 'presenting' versus 'sharing'
- c pupils joining in construction of lines of thought. Cognitive strategies?
- d how social relations are organised and managed
- e the effects of your own participation

   (iv)   Identification of significant episodes that exemplify a-e above. What features are you using as evidence? Are your interpretations of these features shared by other teachers in your work group?

   (v)   Listening to the recording along with the children. Do they share your judgments and interpretations of what was said?

Chapter 4

FRAMES: HOW TO UNDERSTAND CONVERSATIONS

Our attempt to set up category systems for questions and for other formal characteristics of dialogue led us to consider the nature and status of the meanings generated during conversation, and the relation of these meanings to the linguistic forms used. We take the view that meaning should not be taken to adhere to an isolated utterance, but should be seen to arise from the tacit knowledge of participants which they use to attribute meaning to what is said. Different participants bring different bodies of knowledge to the discussion, and at different moments treat one or another sub-system of knowledge as relevant to understanding what is being said. These sub-systems we call 'frames' because they provide for each participant the frames of reference within which his own and other people's utterances are assigned relevance and meaning.

Whenever an investigator categorises an utterance, or assigns a descriptive meaning to it, he necessarily makes assumptions not only about the availability of meanings to an outside observer, but even about the status of these meanings to participants in the conversation. In analysing small group discussions it seems particularly necessary to make explicit what assumptions one is making about the construction and availability of meaning. The problems involved in attributing meaning can best be presented through an example.

Before reading on, the reader may care to see what sense he can make unaided of the following extract from a dialogue.

It's like a diving, diving suit in't it?
Yeah... it's full of air
It's only full of air so he can breathe
No it, it keeps, it stops the er
There's so much pressure when he gets down
Yeah
It stops, it stops it from pushing it in
I wonder how fish and all them survive down there then

Our ability to make any sense at all of what is said depends upon knowledge of deep sea diving equipment and its functions. But this alone is not enough. When we take part in conversation we take for granted our knowledge of the people we are talking to and the probable purposes that the conversation is carrying out, yet without such knowledge we should find it difficult to understand what was said.

The reader did not know that these were three thirteen-year-old school boys discussing a question set to them by a teacher. These boys had been applying their knowledge of air pressure to the question: 'What would happen to the spaceman if he stepped out into space without a space suit on?' It is while they are discussing the space suit that Barry says: 'It's like a diving, diving suit, in't it?' The reader may care now to re-read the passage in the light of this new information, in particular asking himself what the pronoun 'it' refers to upon its various occurrences. (We provide below a parallel commentary which we see as hypothetical, as less than adequate to the complex of meanings available to participants, and as necessarily involving the use of our own knowledge. It seems a useful strategy, however, temporarily to treat some areas of meaning as determinate in order to focus attention on the indeterminacy of others.)

35 Graham: Yeah... it's full of air

'It' seems here to refer to the space suit, but since being 'full of air' is a characteristic shared by the diving suit there is a potential ambiguity present.

36 Barry: It's only full of air so he can breathe

The reference here is entirely ambiguous. As is normal in conversation, however, the ambiguity does not in the least check the exchange.

37 Graham: No it, it keeps, it stops the er

Graham must be attributing a meaning to Barry's 'it' since he begins to contradict the statement, but whether he himself is referring to space suit or diving suit remains as indeterminate to us as to the other two boys (unless we look at his later attempt at No. 40).

38 Alec: There's so much pressure when he gets down

Here we apply our knowledge retrospectively. 'When he gets down' must (we say) mean into the depths of the sea, so Alec (who here speaks for the first time) has identified the 'it' of the two preceding utterances as the diving suit.

39 Barry: Yeah

Barry now adds his support to this identification that is gradually taking shape.

40 Graham:	It stops, it stops it from pushing it in	Graham has now abandoned 'it' = space suit and tacitly accepts the alternative identification. He also introduces a second referent for 'it' and we use our tacit knowledge to identify this as the pressure in the depths of the sea.
41 Barry:	I wonder how fish and all them survive down there then	This tacit identification is used by Barry as a springboard for a venture into a new topic.

The purpose of this analysis has been not merely to point out the way in which complex structures of tacit knowledge (both of the social context and of the matters referred to) are used with great rapidity during conversation in attributing meaning to what is said. More important, perhaps, is the observation that these meanings are fluid and indeterminate (1) - for the participants as much as for the observer. The gradual translation of the referent of 'it' from the space suit to the diving suit through a period of indeterminacy is here intended to illustrate similar processes which go on in all conversations. Participants in conversation continuously attribute both referential meanings and purposes (social meanings) to the ongoing utterances; as we have seen, these interpretations gradually modulate, usually without the speakers being aware of it.

The indeterminacy here enables the boys briefly to try out a possible relationship between space suits and diving suits before moving to another topic, and this is characteristic of how meaning develops during the flux of conversation. In understanding conversation it is important not to impose on it expectations of logical discreteness drawn from some kinds of written language. Talk is different in kind.

We now turn to the sources of this meaning, which lie in the knowledge which the participants bring to the conversation. It is Garfinkel (2) who has been pre-eminently responsible for drawing attention to this. He asks his students to take down a few sequential utterances from a real conversation with an intimate, and beside each utterance to write as for an outsider the meaning which each of these has for the participants. He does this to turn their attention to the implicit knowledge which they use whenever they understand what someone says. This does not mean that there is a body of knowledge which is in some objective sense relevant to interpreting each utterance: there is no determinate meaning for an observer to look for. Thus Garfinkel does not point to a single finite body of knowledge that is relevant to the understanding of an utterance, but intends his students to discover that this knowledge is infinite in that there is no way of limiting what is potentially relevant. We are concerned to add to Garfinkel's concern the idea that each participant as he 'understands' will use a different body of knowledge that for him will be 'relevant'.

In the extract quoted above, the boys use continually changing bodies of knowledge to interpret what is going on in the conver-

sation. The first utterance comes from Barry, who generates it by
mapping his intentions on to a set of linguistic forms which from
his point of view represent them. This utterance is interpreted by
Graham who, using a body of knowledge which he considers relevant,
assigns a meaning to the words spoken. On the basis of this
interpretation of Barry's utterance, Graham replies by selecting the
form of words that constitute the second utterance. That is,
Graham's reply incorporates an implicit interpretation of Barry's
utterance and with it an unspoken context to which it would be relevant. When Barry hears what Graham has said, he in his turn
interprets the words by attributing to Graham a frame of understanding which they share. In speaking the third utterance he generates
a new intention that incorporates a view of what has gone on before,
a view not only of what Graham meant but also of what Graham had
thought he (Barry) had meant in the first utterance. Neither of
them does what Garfinkel's students do in spelling out what they can
of the implied meanings. Barry and Graham engage in their exchange
on the basis of a common assumption of operating in the same frame
of reference, of using the same body of knowledge in understanding
one another. They engage in an act of joint confidence, since even
when competing for control they tacitly assume that they are playing
the same game for the same stakes.

From an observer's point of view, replaying the conversation at
leisure, it may appear that they have at times attributed intentions
falsely to one another, but this itself may be misleading. The very
indefiniteness of the 'meanings' or 'intentions' - their lack of reflective definition, that is - allows participants in discussion to
collaborate in developing a thread of meaning which may change many
times, and radically, in the course of talk.

How do these meanings relate to the form of words used? At their
heart will probably be certain significances which most adult
English speakers would assign to the verbal forms spoken. There may
however be more special meanings which Barry, Graham and Alec can
assign to these words in this context because they have previously
been members of groups who used these words in such contexts for
special purposes, for special meanings referential or expressive.
There may be meanings unique to Barry alone, because of his unique
experiences elsewhere. And so on, according to the range of each
boy's social experiences.

It seems likely that we approach utterances with preconceptions
about 'the kind of things people like X tend to mean in situations
like Y'. If the utterance is familiar we slot it easily into a
frame of readymade interpretations. If it doesn't fit - if we don't
recognise parts of it, or find it out of context or out of role - we
must apply other frames from our experience, sometimes even by constructing a special frame for it. ('The poor chap isn't quite right
in the head', perhaps.)

Both the forms of words and the frames of knowledge are essential
to meaning. Barry's words 'It's only full of air so he can breathe'
do not in themselves have a determinate meaning. However, unless
Graham's past history has led him to assign meanings to these words
which are at least similar to Barry's and Alec's, then the three
cannot communicate.

Barry, Graham and Alec bring their own histories to the interpre-

tation of what goes on in their conversation, histories which themselves contain inconsistencies. Indeed, a person's history may
offer him several interpretative frames which he can select from.
However, as a group they have a history too, since in the course of
interaction, however brief, they are constructing common meanings.
To take an extreme example, some long-standing groups generate
catch-phrases which for them carry implications which are closed to
everyone else. But all groups in a lesser degree set up unique
meanings, though they may in many cases be impermanent.

What is the status of these 'intentions' and 'interpretations'?
It has been said (3) that they have no existence except in so far as
the participants reconstruct them later in reflection, yet this can
hardly be true since the very coherence of a conversational text (as
interpreted by an observer) warrants the presence of some common
understanding. Compare, for example, a section from such a conversational text with a collection of utterances which have been listed
at random. Moreover, any retrospective account would be very
different from the shadowy and half-formed meanings which momentari-
ly shape the exchange. It seems necessary therefore to distinguish
'operational' meanings from 'reflective' meanings.

A participant in a conversation can attend to only part of what
is going on. What is going on includes his interpretation of what
has already been said, both from the point of view of its content
and of its implications for social relationships; these interpretations depend on knowledge which he already holds of the speaker,
the subject-matter, the situation, and the norms of discourse. It
includes also his memory of what he himself has said before, the
scanning of possible replies he might make, and the reading of non-
verbal signals, including those from participants who are not at
that moment speaking. And these constitute only a part of what he
is capable of attending to: extraneous features also impinge on
him, such as whether he is cold or warm. (4)

Most of these events are held only in the short-term memory,
except for those which, because of their significance, are trans-
ferred to the long-term memory. However, they are not stored 'raw',
as they first 'happened', but are reworked during the course of the
conversation. Thus there may be a time lag between Barry's making
an utterance and Graham's responding negatively to that utterance,
the situation, Barry's facial expression, etc. Finally, he interprets the utterance as sarcastic and aggressive: some time later
(maybe some utterances later) he responds accordingly.

Thus, throughout a conversation, Speaker-hearers do not only
'speak' and 'hear', but they also construct a cumulative and idio-
syncratic account of what has been going on. This account is a
construction in that many events are excluded from it, and it is
made of interpretations of events, rather than the events themselves. This business of constructing an account of what happened
in a conversation does not necessarily end when the talking stops
and the conversers separate: it continues when participants reflect
upon what was said. Any account of natural conversation would have
to take account of this. For some conversations, it may be that
much of the meaning of the events is constructed like this, after
the conversation is over. But even this is not fixed: the reflective meaning is always open to change because of new information

available, or new insights achieved by the speaker-hearer as he reflects on events that are past, or talks about them to others.

Thus the observer who seeks to analyse conversations is faced
with highly indeterminate data. It is not merely that he has difficulty in 'understanding' what is said, but that meaning does not
adhere to the utterances themselves. In the act of replying,
participants tacitly attribute meaning to all that has gone before,
but these meanings are normally fluid, partly unfocussed, and liable
to change. The observer is compelled to reconstruct strings of
cumulative reinterpretations in the knowledge that even at the
moment the words were spoken they may have had no determinate
meaning to those who spoke them.

We have put forward a view of what it is that the observer under-
takes to reconstruct, but so far we have confined our attention
mainly to the content of what is said. During every conversation,
however, the participants must not only operate as if they shared
one another's understanding of the matter discussed, but must also
negotiate how they will relate to one another in discussing it.
'Negotiate' may prove a misleading metaphor, since the social
meanings put forward and accepted or rejected are at least as indeterminate and ambiguous as the referential meanings so far discussed. In order to deal with these two kinds of meaning we propose
that every utterance in a conversation should be said to offer two
Frames: (5) one, the Content Frame, offers an interpretation of the
subject in hand, while the other, the Interaction Frame, offers an
interpretation of the social relationships which are shaping the
interaction. We shall approach this obliquely by way of the route
which we ourselves took in formulating these concepts.

Our first approaches to the analysis of small group talk were
coloured by our previous experience of analysing teacher-class dialogue. By virtue of his role a teacher claims the right and responsibility of exercising control over the subject-matter of
lessons and over the patterns of communication. For much of the
time, most pupils accept this right and responsibility as normal.
To take a real example, when a teacher in a science practical lesson
asks a pupil, 'And so what? What beyond that? What's this got to
do with atoms?' he is enacting his right to control. He is indicating that he wants the pupil to link what he has just said with
ideas about atoms; moreover, he probably does not want just any
ideas but particular ideas presented during an earlier lesson. At
the same time he is making it clear that the pupil has no option but
to attempt to answer this question: the pupil's next move is firmly
laid down for him, whatever his private wishes, his role in that
context being progressively defined for him.

Since the public signalling of his purposes is part of a
teacher's accepted role, it is easy to provide a description of the
teacher's utterance quoted above. Since pupil and teacher alike for
the most part tacitly accept that it is the teacher's responsibility
to define the nature of what is going on in a lesson, it is not
difficult to arrive at an account of teachers' moves that would be
acceptable to most observers. This is not to deny that from an observer's point of view the meaning of what a teacher does is often
problematic, but to suggest that there are familiar descriptions of
teaching moves which command ready assent. Thus it is possible to

provide acceptable descriptions (6) of a teacher's contributions to
lessons by attending to the teacher's overt purposes and ignoring
the possibility that what he said meant something different to the
pupils addressed. The acceptability of such descriptions depends on
the teacher's role as director of the interaction being highly
defined and generally unchallenged.

As soon as one turns to small groups where the participants are
of equal status this is no longer the case. In the conversations
which we are considering, each participant tries to guide the dialogue in the direction he wishes, but none lays claim to it as of
right, because none of them has any special rights over the others.
A by-product of such a situation is that the interaction may be
directed away from competition for control, and towards the collaboration needed for the group jointly to carry out their task. The
subject-matter, the way it is approached, the order of speaking, and
the participants' relative influence upon these are all decided by
negotiation, not claimed and conceded as part of a role. One participant's view of what is going on is no more valid than another's.
This interplay between alternative frames of reference constitutes
the social reality which our account seeks to describe.

In order to deal with this multisemic character of dialogue we
wish to propose a theoretical construct which we shall call Frame.
(7) Every time a participant in dialogue makes an utterance he
offers to the other participant two Frames, one referring to
subject-matter which will be called Content Frame and the other referring to the interactive relationship and called Interaction
Frame.

Briefly, by Content Frame we mean this: When Participant A
speaks, his utterance, for him, carries with it a framework of
implicit relevant knowledge, and this constitutes the Offered
Content Frame. Participant B 'understands' this utterance by attributing it to a framework of implicit relevant knowledge, and this
constitutes an Attributed Content Frame. Participant C will understand the same utterance by similarly assigning it to a frame of
reference, another Attributed Content Frame. Thus in the example
cited at the beginning of this chapter we saw the boys move from a
roughly shared Content Frame referring to space suits into a Frame
referring to diving suits. The importance of the shift of Frame is
that it constitutes a shift in the realm of tacit knowledge needed
for understanding. 'It stops it from pushing it in' gains much of
its referential meaning from the 'diving suit' frame.

An Interaction Frame is being offered in the very same utterance
as is the Content Frame, since Participant A's utterance implies
something about the interactive relationship which they are taking
part in. He may make a peremptory demand for a reply, or offer a
hesitant opinion for comment. It may (as in a typical lesson) imply
that the speaker thinks he occupies a role which gives him a positional right to make such a demand; or it may be the expression
of a personal and temporary bid for control. Thus the Interaction
Frame includes both the speaker's attempts to guide the course of
the immediate interaction and his implicit long-term claims to
personal and positional relationships. It is clear that the
speaker's Frames may have more or less relationship to the hearer's
Frames, according to such matters as their degree of common
knowledge, intimacy and so on.

The use of the concept of Frame frees us from any need to assign a determinate and unchanging meaning either to the content of an utterance, or to its significance as a move in the interaction. It aids the observer to deal with (a) the different interpretations held by different participants, (b) the ebb and flow during a conversation between more sharply defined Frames and those moments when Frames are blurred, because in flux or mutually contradictory, (c) the dual aspect of the necessary tacit knowledge, which refers in one direction towards supplying a context for the subject matter and in the other towards a set of expectations about the social meaning of actions. To sum up, Frames refer to participants' implicit expectations about (a) what they are talking about, and (b) their relationships and communicative behaviour. Frames are offered by those who speak and interpreted by those who listen, thus changing in the course of the conversation.

There follows a description of a few minutes of group discussion in which the negotiation of Interaction Frame and Content Frame are separately annotated (see Table 3). The three boys involved are endeavouring to answer questions printed on cards; some of these questions refer to work previously done in a science lesson but others are intended to lead to further thinking about the topic of air pressure. This passage has been chosen because it well illustrates how the Interaction Frame is implicitly presented and modified.

During most of the conversation the boys seem to agree about the nature of the activity they are engaged in. At one point, however, Barry turns to the microphone and says (No.20) 'We've now done two, Tape', thus temporarily embedding the 'group work' activity within a 'tape recording' activity which makes special demands on speakers. This unexpected revision or shift is tacitly accepted by the other boys, just as an expected contribution would have been. To say that they agree about the nature of group work is not to award an ideal or objective status to their conception of it. When Graham reads a question from the card it is treated as a contribution to the task, but it might equally have been the occasion for a joke without the activity ceasing to be group work. The boys determine what constitutes group work by doing it; although their previous school experience plays part in this, the behaviour seen as appropriate is nevertheless open to continuous modification.

Thus the Interaction Frame which is being continually presented and interpreted should not be seen simply as a matrix imposed on the boys' behaviour. It can be represented at three levels of abstraction: the speech event, the speech roles, and the sequences of utterances. In our example, the Frame must include at the level of speech event a view of school tasks, how they should be tackled, and the part that discussion should play in this. This Frame is realised, however, only through the adoption by participants of a series of interrelated speech roles. For example the first part of this sequence is particularly concerned with competition between Graham and Barry, first for the role of gatekeeper (8) (in pacing and giving recognition to the group's progress through the questions) and then for control of the floor in a more diffuse speech role. However, the speech roles themselves are realised in sequences of speech acts; question may be followed by answer, and assertion by

TABLE 3 Analysis into Content and Interaction Frames

Utterance no. and pupil's name	Utterance	Interaction Frame	Content Frame
19 Graham:	Number two, why did the cork come out?	Claiming role of gatekeeper, Graham reads question from task card.	The Content Frame derives from the teacher who wrote the task card, which refers to an earlier lesson and to the frame then set up.
	We've done that, haven't we?	Gatekeeping and asking for approval of his gatekeeping move.	They assume a common frame and the content here switches momentarily to their conduct of the task.
20 Barry:	Yeah, we've done that	Confirms Graham's move.	Conduct of task.
	We've now done two, Tape	Addresses tape recorder, making tacit assumptions that the recorder audience is not part of the group and does not share group meanings.	Conduct of task.
	All right, if a piece of rock hit a spaceship and made a hole in, what would happen to the air?	Taking over the gatekeeping role, Barry signals a change of topic, and reads a new question (Question 3).	Although chosen by the teacher, this question has not been discussed before and so is open to interpretation.

All't air would come roo, rushing out wouldn't it? Er, all the air would come rushing out.	Answers question, asking for support, but excluding others from the floor.	Assumes sufficient consensus about the Content Frame implied in the question for a brief answer, without detailed explication, to be acceptable.
* What would happen to the spaceman if he stepped out into space without a space suit on?	Reads next question (No.4), still acting as gatekeeper.	This question from the teacher is also open to interpretation.
21 Alec: Would suck everything out with it.	Challenges Barry's monopoly of the floor (both speaking at once).	Specifies as relevant to Question 3 details not mentioned by Barry, thus imposing a modification of the implicit Content Frame.
22 Barry: Oh, he'd, he, all, all his, all his body would explode	Trying to hold the floor.	Briefly indicates a Frame.
23 Graham: He'd explode	Competing for the floor.	Has now accepted move to Question 4. Frame so far common with Barry.
24 Barry: He'd expand, wouldn't he? He'd explode	Competing for the floor.	Adds alternative construction to Frame.
25 Graham: He'd just explode because erm, he's got pressure from inside the space ship inside him	Competing for the floor.	Explicates the Frame he is offering by beginning to analyse process.

	Utterance		
26 Barry:	[Yeah, yeah, he's not used to it really is he?	Weakening his ploy with elements of acknowledgment and appeal.	Barry explicates part of his Frame.
27 Graham:	Well even so, even if he breathed out or something like that there's	Graham has captured the floor.	Implicitly rejects part of Barry's frame on the basis of the previous utterance. Rejects possibility of adaptation to pressure, i.e. contradicting Barry's 'Not used to it'.
28 Barry:	[Yeah	Barry reduced to supporting role.	Preparing to accept Graham's Frame.
29 Graham:	Still't pressure that he's used to, inside him and there in't any pressure outside at all, so he gets, he just explodes	Holds the floor.	Continues to expound own Frame in detail (without indicating whether its status is hypothetical).
30 Barry:	Yeah.... How, does a pace, space suit stop it? Is there air inside?	Asks for information, thus implicitly conceding expertise to Graham. (N.B. Alec has remained silent ever since his original challenge at No.21 to Barry's control of the interaction.)	Abandons own Frame and tries to grasp Graham's Frame.

* Brackets indicate simultaneous speech.

qualification or rebuttal, the nature of these categories and their appropriate sequencing being open to ad hoc interpretation by the participants. For example, the attempts to capture the floor (Nos 20-28) are realised by a series of simultaneous and related assertions. Barry's loss of the initiative is realised by his weak 'Yeah' (at No.28) and by his question 'How does a pace, space suit stop it? Is there air inside?' (No.30) which can be taken to concede expertise to Graham. Although we are here assigning a description to these utterances this is no more than an attempt to reconstruct from our understanding of the context the meaning most likely to have been understood and acted upon by other participants. The utterances, as they are sequenced, constitute interlocking speech roles which can be interpreted as the speech event 'group work'; our understanding of the interaction (whether as participants or observers) operates as much from utterances upwards as from 'group work' downwards.

If we compare Graham's 'He'd just explode because erm, he's got pressure from inside the spaceship inside him' (No.25), with Barry's nearly simultaneous 'Yeah, yeah, he's not used to it really, is he?' (no.26) there seems to be a difference in the manner in which these two utterances present their interlocking Interaction Frames. Graham seems at this point to be making an unambiguous claim to the right to give explanations. Barry's 'Yeah, yeah', on the other hand, sounds to an outsider to be an over-eager concession to the opinion expressed by Graham, and the final tag-question 'Is he?' is a request for support which could be described as insecure. That is, the proposal of an Interaction Frame may be made strongly or weakly. At this moment in the exchange Barry is presenting his claim to the dominant speech role weakly. We shall therefore speak of a Weak or Strong Interaction Frame, though this is a characteristic which we attribute only to Presented Frames. At the level of sequential utterances (at the third level described in the previous paragraph) Barry next proposes a much stronger Interaction Frame when he asks 'How does a pace, space suit stop it?', since this indicates clearly that he expects an informative reply from Graham. We can compare this with No.22 'Oh he'd, he, all his, all his body would explode', which leaves open the kind of response which would be approximate (in terms of Interaction Frame, not in terms of content).

Just as the Interaction Frame can be presented in Stronger and Weaker forms, so can Content Frames. When Barry asks 'How does a pace, space suit stop it?' (No.20), this enacts not only his sense of the group's relationship (that is, presents an Interaction Frame) but also proposes a redirection of their subject. The knowledge related to space suits still underlies their common understanding, but Barry is directing their attention to a particular issue; he wants them to explain the efficacy of space suits in the light of their (assumed) understanding of the effects of pressure. Thus Barry's question offers a strong Content Frame since it sets out to focus their attention more sharply on a particular issue.

Throughout this episode - or at least since Barry's address to the tape recorder in No.20 - the Content Frame has been progressively clarified. In answer to the teacher's written question 'What would happen to the spaceman if he stepped out into space without a

space suit on?' both Barry and Graham reply (Nos 22 and 23) that he
would explode. It becomes clear as the exchange continues, however,
that the implicit Content Frames being presented by the two boys are
not identical; that is, the Content Frames become stronger until
their lack of fit becomes apparent to the speakers. Barry presents
a view of pressure ('He's not used to it really') which causes
Graham (in 27 and 29) to contradict him, and offer another account.
At this point Barry gives way, and from 28 onwards the discussion is
based upon a tacit agreement that they share a Content Frame, that
is, that all are using the same bodies of knowledge and context of
relevance.

In a school context of this kind it is not surprising to find a
predominance of utterances offering Strong Content Frames, since the
clarifying of content constitutes the manifest function of the discussion. If Graham had instead sought to alter the function of the
talk by saying with a vague gesture 'What do you think of all this?'
he would be offering a Weak Content Frame, since both 'What' and
'this' are open to a wide range of interpretations. Weak Content
Frames of this kind are likely to be common in informal conversations at those points when people wish to talk but not to express
strong preferences for particular subject-matter. (Strength of
Frames is discussed in more detail in Chapter 5.)

Influence of content upon interaction - and vice versa - is to be
expected, since most of the interaction in our example is concerned
with the control of content. For example, when Barry says (No.20)
'All't air would come roo, rushing out wouldn't it?' the tag-
question 'wouldn't it?' invited agreement or disagreement. Expressions of modality (such as 'wouldn't it?' spoken with certain
intonations) implicitly acknowledge the possibility of alternative
relevances. Thus, although the Content Frame is Strong, the Weak
Interaction Frame indicates willingness to discuss alternatives.
Barry is not claiming a unique right to decide what is relevant.
(If a teacher spoke a similar sentence in a lesson he would be
likely to do so with an intonation which turned the 'wouldn't it?'
into a demand for agreement; that is, teachers usually lay a positional claim to the right to decide what is relevant.)

In this chapter we have put forward the view that the meaning of
an utterance lies not in the utterance itself but in the implicit
hypotheses about it which shape the future history of the conversation. Meanings are characteristics of people not of utterances,
or - to be more precise - are attributed by people to utterances in
context. (10) Participants in communication understand an utterance
in terms of the Content and Interaction Frames which they ascribe to
it, that is in terms of 'knowledge of how things are' which they
bring to it. Since these frames are seldom made explicit they are
seldom explicitly rebutted. (One can, however, imagine someone
saying, 'I'm not talking about supermarkets; it was the open air
market.') The Frames utilised by participants in understanding a
particular utterance are seldom explicitly confirmed or denied in
informal conversation, since such explicitness would alter the
nature of the speech event. Instead they are implicitly and gradually confirmed in part, reshaped in part, and thus move on - as we
have shown - from one state to another. It is thus entirely inappropriate for an observer to search for a determinate meaning in the

form of an utterance or in the responses of an idealised hearer or
a typical informant; its meaning lies both in the operational
meaning, and in the subsequent history of that speech event and its
participants, and nowhere else.

As observers, therefore, we have no more right than any participant to ascribe meanings to what is said. Nevertheless, the study
of talk necessitates statements about meaning; without them we
cannot discuss our subject-matter. This requires us to adopt the
role of the 'ideal observer', in that we aim to represent some
aspects of the meaning as it may have been interpreted by participants. We remain aware that our construction of meaning is hypothetical and that it cannot in its nature represent meaning as
multiple and infinite. As observers, however, we have a privileged
position in comparison with the reader, because of our detailed
knowledge of the children and of the circumstances of the
recordings, and because we had the opportunity to listen repeatedly
to passages from the tapes.

The theoretical position taken up in this paper prescribes limits
to the use made of data of this kind. For example, in categorising
discourse moves the observer uses his own Frames to attribute
meaning to the utterances. If the quantitative results of the
categorising are then used as a basis for statements about cognitive
or social events, the validity of these statements rests upon the
appropriateness of the Frames used, that is, upon the observer's
ability to reconstruct in imagination the participants' knowledge of
the world and of talk as they are using it at that moment in the
conversation. It is well for any researcher in the field to ponder
the implications of this.

Chapter 5

QUESTIONS AND QUESTIONING

We became interested in the role played by questions in learning talk when, early in the project's life, we first considered how children collaborated with one another in the course of constructing shared meanings. Since each child brings a differing set of frames to the problem at issue, each approaches it from a perspective which is in some respects unique. If the members of a group are to advance their understanding of the problem through talk, these differences of perspective must be interrelated and their discontinuities used to generate new and more inclusive understanding. It seemed to us likely that groups would differ in the extent to which they supported an individual member's attempts to relate other children's viewpoints to their own, and to use the other's viewpoint in problem-solving. We expected that such a negotiation between differing viewpoints would play an important part in any learning which went on during group discussion. Awareness of the validity of a divergent perspective might reasonably be expected to make one's own perspective appear hypothetical rather than absolute, and therefore open to modification. The effectiveness of such negotiation would depend upon those devices whereby members of the group ask for one another's opinions, encourage explicitness, pinpoint differences, interrelate viewpoints, and so on. It seemed to us that questions were a prime means of performing all of these, and this was why we turned our attention to them.

This chapter attempts three tasks. First we consider some methods of analysing questions put forward by linguists and philosophers and discuss the relationship between question forms and questioning functions. Then we turn to cognitive aspects of questioning and examine the possibility, put forward by some psychologists, that some question forms are superior to others as strategies for obtaining and organising knowledge. Finally, we consider how questioning plays a part in situations where some participants have power over others, and relate this briefly to our group discussions and how questions are used in them.

1   QUESTION FORMS AND QUESTIONING FUNCTIONS

Earlier linguists who looked at questions made question identification, and formal classification the focus of their work. There
is fairly general agreement on formal signs by which questions may
be identified. Otto Jespersen, (1) for instance, describes the
following four formal features, none of which taken alone are an
absolute sign that any given utterance is a question, but of which
two or three would combine in something that we would readily recognise as such. The features are:

1 The use of special interrogative words, such as 'why', 'when',
   'how', etc.
2 Intonation
3 Word Order, namely the placing of the subject in relation to
   the verb
4 The use of the word 'do', as in 'Do you live here?'

The treatment of other grammarians (2) is very similar, although
there are differences in terminology.
    It is important to note that linguists also distinguish a further
question-form. This is the Appended or Tag-question (as in 'You
live there, don't you?'), which is thought of as having several
other functions besides that of interrogation. For instance, a tag-
question is claimed to function as a request to the person addressed
to confirm a statement just made, or to express the speaker's
reaction to a previous statement. Information about the precise
function a tag-question is performing is thought to be carried
formally by its intonational features, that is, by its tune. (3)
    More recently Bolinger considered some of the problems involved
in defining questions:
    The question is an entity that is often assumed, but seldom de-
    fined... The difficulty of definition betokens a complex which
    is not only made up of a number of ingredients, but whose in-
    gredients may vary as to the presence or absence of proportionate
    weight... For persons who demand rigorous definitions, the term
    Question cannot be defined satisfactorily so as to include the
    types that they themselves would spontaneously identify as
    questions.
As a result of this, Bolinger used the strategy of confining himself
to instances 'which the average speaker would unreflectingly label
questions'. (4)
    Huddleston (5) says that questions are divided into two kinds on
the basis of three sets of criteria, but points out that these sets
of criteria do not always correspond. The criteria are:

1 Presuppositions - whether the whole of the information in the
   question is in doubt, or only part of it
2 Form - whether a WH-interrogative word is present or not
3 Expected answer - whether a yes/no answer is adequate or a
   more complex answer is required

In using criteria of kinds 1 and 3 Huddleston is clearly going
beyond the formal characteristics of questions and involving the

linguist in interpretive judgments: the matters which we have discussed within the concept 'frame' would therefore be relevant to
Huddleston's identification of questions.

Since Huddleston's book is based on a corpus of written language,
he is not faced with discussing the functions of questions in spoken
discourse, though he does note that in written texts rhetorical
questions are used to define the topic of a passage. Huddleston,
like other recent linguists, has adopted the term 'illocutionary
force' which the philosophers Austin (6) and Searle (7) have used to
describe the functional value given to an utterance. Huddleston
contrasts the mood of a sentence (e.g. 'interrogative') with the
illocutionary force (e.g. 'question') of that same sentence viewed
as an utterance. He adds, however: 'We should expect the
illocutionary force of an utterance to be largely if not wholly
explicable in terms of the semantic-syntactic description of the
accompanying sentence.' This may be true of Huddleston's corpus of
text; our own conversational data would tend not to conform to his
expectation.

Some linguists use the term 'situation' in dealing with the phenomena that our concept of 'frame' is intended to deal with. For
example, Quirk and Greenbaum write in their recent university
textbook: 'Questions are usually prompted by what was said before,
though they may be stimulated by the situational context' (8) This
seems somewhat misleading: such initiating questions do not always
arise from anything so publicly produceable as a 'situation', but
from the purposes and knowledge - sometimes entirely private - which
participants bring to the occasion. The main discussion of
questions in Quirk and Greenbaum's book is, however, unlike
Huddleston's account of question, entirely concerned with question
forms; the relation of form with function is not mentioned.

Our own interest in questions arose from attempts to categorise
our data. But we had at this stage already transcribed our
recordings and in the course of transcription decisions had been
made about what utterances were questions. The secretary who did
the transcribing had included question marks as part of her standard
punctuation, and the researcher who checked the transcriptions had
accepted or altered or added to these as part of the checking
process. Therefore, the initial decisions which judged certain
utterances to be questions were made on the basis of the intuitional
knowledge available to these two people as speaker-hearers. And at
this stage, we did not seem to have any problems with the identification of questions. Indeed, on scanning through the transcripts,
with the identifying criteria from the literature in mind, it seemed
that there was a remarkable agreement between these intuitional
judgments, and ones that would have been made purely on the basis of
these criteria.

It is precisely this intuitional knowledge that has been drawn on
by linguists in their analysis of questions. The difficulties
Bolinger draws attention to are not difficulties in spotting
questions, and responding to them, during the course of interaction:
this is viewed as easy. What is difficult is accounting openly for
how one does this, and drawing up a list of the criteria which one
responds to. Bolinger has pointed out that linguists have differed
in what criteria they have included. It is important to note that

when we were making our decisions about the allocation of question
marks to utterances, we had available to us both what went before,
and what came after, each utterance. Utterances were not judged
alone, apart from the fabric of on-going social interaction. We had
knowledge of what had gone before, and these previous utterances
generated interpretive schemes which influenced our judgment of
later ones.

Another set of intuitional judgments were also made with regard
to intonational criteria for the identification of questions. There
are of course, standard works which can be consulted on the interpretations that can typically be assigned to the different
'tunes' in which a given phrase may be uttered. However, David
Crystal (9) has made the point that intonation itself is not absolute, but must be interpreted; that is, meanings do not exist 'out
there' somewhere for different intonational tunes, but are made in
the minds of the hearers. This was brought home to us very clearly
when listening to our tapes. For the standard 'tunes' are based
upon a model speaker who uses standard English. The speech of the
children we recorded had many local dialect features, however, and
in particular a phonology that is peculiar to this corner of the
world. It seems to us that intonation is closely related to the
phonological and articulatory features of the sounds actually produced. Put less abstractly, this means that the 'tunes' for 'isn't
it?' (as given is, say, O'Connor and Arnold (10)) sound different
from the tunes for 'innit?' or ''nit?' To assign a function to such
localised forms, we had to use what we had in the way of locally
attuned ears; when baffled, we were helped by the project's secretary, who was often able to 'translate' both phrases and 'tunes'
that were opaque to us.

Despite small differences of opinion on the criteria to be used
in the identification of an utterance as a question, linguists have
at least agreed in the belief that questions exist, and that there
is something about questions that makes them different from other
utterances. Philosophers, however, who have also paid attention to
questions, have differed in their views on this, and there is a
whole school of thought that holds that questions are really
statements.

Perhaps the most extended treatment of this theme is Harrah's,
(11) whose aim is to construct a model of the way a rational
'Receiver' evaluates sequences of messages by attending to their
semantic and pragmatic properties. The emphasis is on the word
'rational', for the model of man presumed in Harrah's analysis is
rooted in assumptions about rationality that are made in game theory
and decision theory. Implicit in this is the notion that the
Receiver wants to gain as much information as possible for as little
cost as possible (whilst also evaluating the worth of the Sender as
an information source). Harrah explores the way this rational man
would ask questions, and what he would allow as acceptable answers.
In doing so, he concludes that questions can be better viewed as
statements, for this then makes them available to the logic of truth
functions, and of the predicate calculus.

He comments that other philosophers, notably Wittgenstein and
Hamblin, unite in defence of the idea that questions are somehow
different from statements. His own theory is diametrically opposed

to this: 'We shall construe questions as statements, and regard the logic of questions as already existing in the logic of statements.' And again,

> Our basic notion is in reinterpretation of the question and answer process. In this reinterpretation, the question and answer situation is construed not as a sequence of requests and satisfactions, but as a game played with statements, specifically, an information matching game. Information seeking questions are regarded as tools for reducing states of rational doubt...

The advantage of viewing questions as statements is that they then become susceptible to the operations of symbolic logic and the predicate calculus; that is, the statement seen as inherent in the question can be assigned a truth value. This idea of treating questions as statements seems to be not a new one. It was mooted by Waisman, (12) for instance, before the 1940s, although its exposition in a revised form was not published until 1965. However, Harrah's seems to be the first attempt to work out analytically the implications of treating questions like this.

Harrah's model of communication focusses upon the exchange of information. For him, a question constitutes a presentation of information just as much as a statement does, and a question differs from a statement in that it also contains within it an invitation to reply. We have found this view of questioning behaviour useful because it has helped us to understand how a group builds up a shared view of a topic. When someone asks a question he offers an implicit definition of the boundaries of the subject discussed. Take, for example, this question asked early in a discussion of Steinbeck's nouvelle 'The Pearl' (the children had read only the early part of the book):

> 'What do you think that'll happen later on in the book, when we've read it, you know, what will happen to the pearl, and to the doctor and everything? Will it all turn out happily, and that, or will, you know, somebody die or something like that?'
> (Marianne in Group 1 talking about 'The Pearl').

This question proposes strict limits for the range of relevant replies: the other children are first invited to make predictions, then these predictions are given some specific reference to 'the pearl, and the doctor and everything', and then the range of appropriate replies is narrowed still further towards happy endings or (as a contrast apparently) someone's death. Thus the question sets up a Content Frame which implicitly constrains what follows in the conversation. (This appears to be what Harrah means when he treats questions as statements.) The other members of the group may ignore the Frame presented in the question, they may adopt and develop it, or they may adapt and change it. If they adopt or adapt the Frame it becomes part of the implicit shared knowledge which will underlie the remainder of their discussion of the topic. Thus Harrah's view helps us to understand how questions contribute to the construction of knowledge in dialogue.

However, the exchange or construction of knowledge is not the sole function of dialogue. Harrah uses a model of man as a rational game-player, seeking as much information as he can for as little payment as possible. Yet there are very cogent reasons why we should be wary of construing natural questioning behaviours within

such a model. Perhaps most important is that information-seeking is
only one of the reasons why people ask questions. Our conversations
are as much concerned with our social relationships as with the
information which we share. Even the most task-oriented discussion
depends upon the successful ordering of discourse; at the same time
as the topic is discussed the participants must decide who is to
speak and for how long, must negotiate change of speaker, and engage
in collaboration, or conflict, or both. To focus solely on the
informational aspect of questions is to reduce question asking and
answering to their content alone: question-asking then becomes like
looking something up in a dictionary. But we have relationships
with other people which it is not possible to maintain with a
dictionary. In other words, questioning is a social act, not simply
one pertaining to the individual's cognitions.

Our emphasis on the importance of interactional features of
question marks the point where we part company with Harrah, but
this does not mean that we return to the standard formulation that
'Whatever else we know, one thing we know for sure - questions are
not statements'. (13)

We concede that there are some utterances which any hearer would
unhesitatingly describe as questions. What seems to be happening
in such utterances is that they not only present a Content Frame,
but that they also explicitly resign possession of the floor to
someone else, sometimes indicating which person. Utterances like
this seem to say 'Message Completed; over to you'. In other words,
as well as the message they carry about relevance of content, they
also carry a message about the social relations of the conversation;
and the specific social message in the case of the archetypal
question form is to indicate the handing over of the speech-role to
another speaker.

But a communication about the social relationship may equally be
made in order to lay claim to, or take over, the speech role. Such
an utterance contains just as much specification of the speech role
as does a 'question', but it may or may not be made in the question
form. We subsume these messages about social relationships within
a conversation under the notion of Interaction Framing, which
parallels our notion of Content Framing.

As we wrote in Chapter 4, utterances vary in the strength with
which they put these frames forward. Utterances which make an
explicit statement about speech roles we think of as putting forward
a strong Interaction Frame, regardless of whether the intention is
to depute someone else to the speech role, or to lay claim to it,
whereas we think of utterances which make no such claim as offering
a very weak Interaction Frame. It will be clear that questions and
statements alike can put forward a strong interaction frame, e.g.
'What do you think Chris' has a strong interaction frame because it
nominates another person to the speech role. Whereas 'Shurrup,
there's a microphone there, I'll smash you' makes an equally strong
claim via a very different form.

Attempts at dominance may also be made or rebuffed via a question
form. For example, when one girl tried to exert control over a boy
with: 'You silly rat, you don't do that', the latter replied in a
challenging tone: 'Who doesn't?' Here the question form was not in
the least acting as a request for information or action; it was an

implicit rejection of the girl's right to tell him what to do. In
groups of children talking together, such strong attempts to control
speech roles are less common that they are in classrooms, where many
teachers claim the management of speech roles as part of their
position and status. Most teachers would see decisions about who
talks, on what topic, and for how long as part of their job.

Forms do not therefore necessarily impose specific functions.
Rather, speaker-hearers choose freely from a number of devices which
carry out varied functions, and they use these forms in an inno-
vative and varied fashion. Forms are shaped to the purpose of
speakers, and not vice-versa.

At this point, we should like to summarise our theory of Frames,
and then go on to use it to analyse some data to show how we operate
it in practice.

We propose that speakers whenever they speak offer Frames for
both Interaction and Content, and that these frames vary in the
strength of their claims. Messages are carried not solely by the
formal status of the utterance as a question or assertion, but by
the strength of the Interaction and Content Frames which are offered. Different forms may carry similar Interactional Frames, that
is, may make equally strong assumptions about speech roles. In our
view, to classify utterances into 'Questions' and 'Assertions' is to
omit from consideration important aspects of what purposes speakers
have for their utterances in conversation.

In practice, the questions/statements typology has derived from
the classification of single utterances considered alone, and out of
context: all of the sources discussed so far consider single
instances of questions, which are often, incidentally, made-up
examples. Yet, as we indicated earlier, we found that to make sense
of any utterance, we had to consider it in its context: we had to
look back at what went before, and forwards to what followed. (Participants in a conversation go through an analogous process. They
make a sense for an utterance related to what has gone before, and
may alter it in response to later events.) Not unnaturally, the
examination of questions out of context does not give any information about the role played by that context in the hearer's gener-
ation of a meaning for the utterance; yet interaction is always
situated: there is no such thing as context-free interaction. If
meaning does not adhere to the actual utterance, but arises from the
interpretation of that utterance in terms of frame, we can hardly
expect to attribute a frame to it without going through a process
that is analogous to the progress of a participant through a conversation.

To show this process in action, we turn to our data.

In the example below, Group 3 are discussing the planning
problems of National Parks, considering especially how to reconcile
the needs of varied uses such as tourism, farming, industry, outdoor
pursuits, and so on. The task card mentions suggestions which have
been made for the provision in the Lake District of cinemas, caravan
sites, restaurants and so on. They have all agreed that cinemas and
night clubs should not be built in the Lakes, when Margaret suddenly
spots something on the task card which she wishes to query:

37 Margaret: Anyhow if they've got a caravan site, what do they want a camping site and all for? And if they've got a restaurant what do they want a re-freshment stall for?
(Laughter)
Well it's true, what do they want them all for?

At first sight, here are three 'Wh' questions; formal analysis would classify these as open questions. Margaret is asking the group what justification there might be for the provision of these facilities. Or is she? She is speaking in an angry tone of voice, and she prefaces the questions with signs that maybe she is not request-ing another point of vi view. Is she asking the group a question, or is she daring them to disa-gree with her?

38 Robert: Well a restaurant's really for people who want to have a meal, an' a, an' a refreshment stall is for people who wanna snack like a hot dog or a drink.

Robert takes a chance on the first interpretation. In modest tones, he shows how restaurants and re-freshment stalls serve different needs, and supplies a justification for the provision of both of them.

39 Christine: Well they can go away

Christine strongly rejects Robert's contri-bution.

40 Margaret: What do they want a kiosk for, just to drink, ugh, it's stupid. What do they want a kiosk for?

Margaret indicates that she sees Robert's reply at 38 not as compliance with her request for reason, but as disa-greement with a view she holds strongly - that these facilities are un-necessary. She rejects this alternative viewpoint most strongly.

41 Robert: Anyway, I don't think there ought to be tennis courts.

Robert has learned his lesson. He is not deceived by the question format of Margaret's 40 again. His attempt at 38 to supply reasons he thought were being re-quested has earned him verbal punishment. Now he changes the subject, implicitly accepting the force of Margaret's Interaction Frame.

We now turn to a group who on this occasion ask each other hardly any questions, but who nevertheless hand over speech roles to each other in a collaborative fashion. Group 1 have read the transcript of an interview with a young delinquent, and they have been asked to discuss 'The Causes of Vandalism'.

3 David: I think the area you live in er, could affect the way they behave because when there's other gangs around you, I think it er, you know make you want to fight too if you see em all, fighting and that, it looks like fun and so he'll just join in

David states that he thinks that peer group influence is a factor in gang violence. There are several markers which indicate that this is a tentatively held view: 'I think', 'er', 'I think it er'. This is not a dogmatic statement with which other participants will disagree at their peril, but an attempt to get the ball rolling. This is a contribution which can be built on and extended, as Jonathan does at 4.

4 Jonathan: Yeah, he only, only, he'll only start fighting if other people do

The 'Yeah' acknowledges David's line of thought before extending it.

5 Marianne: And he thinks that the only way he can make his self, big, and make his self a somebody, is to prove to people that he is, big and is, tough and fight, and can fight all time

Marianne connects her utterance to those preceding with the 'and' and also by further extension of the on-going line of thought.

A little later the same group continues:

15 Marianne: They seem to have their own cafés that they think their own, they own, and nobody else can come in ... but I, I think all this is partly because of his upbringing, and the way he was treat when his, tre-treated when he was little.

16 David: Well I think vandalism is, how it comes about is, they should, should have erm, more facilities for people messing about

17 Jonathan: Yeah, but they just reject these facilities

	because they'll think they're no good, just for puffs and that
18 David:	Yeah. Well I don't, I don't mean like - just like wrecking them. Don't mean like youthclubs, more erm, discoteques and that, where, where over fifteen
19 Jonathan:	Yeah, but all they do is fight there
20 Marianne:	The, they can only go round in big gangs. They don't think of,
21 David:	Well, none of them'll fight by their selves

Through this extract, we hear the exchange of viewpoints about what
the causes of vandalism might be. None of them are stated dogmati-
cally, and no one person either lays explicit claim to the role of
speaker or nominates anyone else to speak. Utterances follow each
other smoothly. After pauses have indicated that one person has
temporarily come to the end of what he has to say, another group
member gives voice to his or her own thoughts. Note how tightly
connected the content of the exchange is. These children are exploring collectively what they know. Where someone disagrees with
the content of a previous utterance as at 17, they make a gentle
qualification, not a full-blown disagreement. None of these
children is trying either to manage the talk, or to get someone else
to take responsibility for it: rather, they share, collaboratively,
in the joint construction of an understanding. Speech roles are
left fluid, such that it is open to any participant to contribute
when he likes, rather than being either nominated to do so or
stopped from doing so by other members. The whole exchange is
carried out by statements. Yet these statements are a very effective way of eliciting another person's viewpoint. Thus, although
a question or statement form functions - all else being equal - as
an interrogative or assertive move, in conversation this information
is frequently overruled by interpretations drawn from the larger
context, many of them unspoken. An overemphasis on forms has re-
sulted from a specific method of analysis, namely the consideration
of isolated utterances only. Our examination of situated continuous
discourse leads us to believe that question and non-question forms
may be used to make similar claims about speech roles, that is, to
offer similar Interaction Frames.

COGNITIVE ASPECTS OF QUESTIONING

We now turn to the part played by questioning in the obtaining and
shaping of knowledge. Previous studies (14) of the questioning
behaviour of children have tended to focus on questions (a) asked by
younger children, which are (b) addressed to adults. It is only to
be expected, therefore, that there should seem to be some quite
marked differences between the conclusions drawn about questioning
behaviour described in such researches, and those that we came to in
our study of the collaborative conversation of secondary school
children. It is useful to trace the development of questions from
their beginnings in early childhood through to adolescence in order
to cast light on the origins of these differences.

   Questioning is usually seen as an attempt by the child to gain

information about matters around him. However, he cannot gain
information by questioning until he has sufficient command of the
necessary language skills to be able to form questions. At its
earliest and simplest stage, this is done by the use of single word
utterances, spoken with rising intonation. These are followed by
simple yes-no questions, that is, questions which are formed by
making only a single transformation. Finally, wh- questions, which
require two transformations, appear. (15)

Although questioning in verbal form cannot be observed until the
child has mastered these verbal forms, it would be misleading to
conclude that the act of inquiry appears only when the child can
say, for instance, 'Daddy gone?' with the appropriate rising intonation. It seems more fruitful to view questioning as a development
of the young child's vocabulary of exploratory behaviours which are
utilised almost from birth. Hildy Ross (16) discusses the role of
looking, listening, touching, and, of course, locomotion in the
baby's exploration of its environment. As each new skill (e.g.
following a moving object with the eyes, finger-thumb opposition,
crawling, walking, etc.) is mastered, it is used by the child for
exploratory purposes. Verbal skills are similarly used for exploration. Verbal questions have the advantage over physical exploration that they bring into the sphere of the child's inquiry
objects, persons and events which are not physically present. He
cannot crawl into yesterday, but he can ask about what he did then.
Questioning, then, can be seen as yet another form of exploratory
behaviour, with curiosity as its underlying motive. However, Ross
(17) also suggests, albeit tentatively, that we could turn this
relationship on its head, and view early visual and tactile exploration of the environment as a primitive form of questioning. She
speculates that such behaviour may be guided by a specific information gap which the infant explorer is seeking to have filled:
'Visual or tactile exploration might then consist of scanning the
stimulus until a particularly relevant piece of information was
found, followed by closer attention to the particular information
that could help to answer the question.'

It is tempting to see in this suggested process the early origin
of Content Frames as we discuss them in Chapter 4. However, underlying Ross's account of questioning and exploration there seems to
be a view of the nature of knowledge. Within this view, the child
has an established structural representation of the world, which is
lacking in one particular. Questioning or exploratory behaviour
serves to supply the information to close this gap.

In contrast with this, Lewis (18) suggests that when the young
child asks questions, he is not necessarily seeking new information,
but may be

practising the formulation of events that he can already tentatively make for himself. He is rapidly building up for himself
a structure of knowledge, a system of symbolisation. He is in-
cited to do this by others in their questions to him;   he
practises question-and-answer in play with them and by himself;
and he often asks questions, the answer to which he already
knows, seeking as it were social approval or rejection of his own
answers. It may be that he is experimenting all the time to discover what may or may not be admitted to his system of knowledge.

> At first this may be half-blind groping by trial and error;
> gradually, through social co-operation, it becomes more clear-
> sighted, and more immediately and effectively directed towards
> its goals.

Lewis's account corresponds more closely to the phenomena which we
have attempted to describe in using the concept of Frame. It seems
as if the young child carries out his exploration not only by a
'dialogue' with the environment but also by matching his existing
representations of the world against those of other people. He
thereby makes alternative constructions available. Thus, though
learning is at times a matter of information closure, there are
occasions when the testing and modifying of whole representational
structures is carried out through dialogue with other people. Such
an account accords with our own view of Content Frames as open to
continuous change in the course of interaction. Understanding
becomes a continuous process rather than a once for all closure.
We have suggested, in Chapter 4, that the offering of Content Frames
by speakers, their interpretation by hearers, and their subsequent
modification (or otherwise) by all participants, constitutes an
aspect of any interactional exchange. It should not surprise us to
find precursors of this complex communicative behaviour already
present in schematic form in the child's exploration of his environment by the locomotive, visual and other means which are characteristic of this early stage of development.

   Not surprisingly, the subject-matter of children's questions
has been one of the features by which they have been frequently
classified (as, for example, in Stanley Hall's early study (19)).
But another approach has been to focus on the forms of the questions
put by children. Since wh- questions are the last to appear, and
since they require more sophisticated transformations than yes-no or
other questions, they have sometimes been presumed to constitute
evidence of a higher level of cognitive ability. In Piaget's study,
(20) the main focus of his interest is on wh- questions, and more
particularly, on why questions. Piaget analysed 1,125 questions
uttered spontaneously by a boy called Del, during the period when
he was aged between six and seven years. (On some days only 'why'
questions were noted down.)

   For Piaget, the kinds of questions Del asks are inextricably
bound up with his transition from pre-causality to causal thought.
This precausality derives from a confusion by the child between
psychological motivation, and the mechanical or physical orderings
of things. It begins at a time (about three years of age) when the
child first becomes aware of the intentions and motivations of the
people around him; an awareness which allows him to predict what
the actions of these people will be. Then, since human actions can
be explained by reference to psychological intent, he applies the
same model to anything that needs explaining. Initially, 'Why' is
a question used for every purpose indiscriminately, because of this
confusion between 'psychological intentionalism' and 'physical
causality'. This kind of why question only decreases as the child
develops an idea of chance, and of some relationships being 'given';
thereafter, 'why' becomes an inappropriate question in some
contexts. Once the idea of chance develops, questions that would
have been put in a 'why' form, are now put as 'how' questions, or

as simple, directly interrogative questions, concerned as much with
the consequences and inner mechanism of the phenomenon as with its
underlying 'cause'. The frequency of 'why' questions, relative to
the total number of questions, decreases during the period 3-7
years, and this decrease is seen by Piaget as 'an index of a
weakening of precausality'. At the same time, there is an increase
in the number of 'why's' which do ask for causal explanation.

Overall, Piaget distinguishes three main groups of 'why'
questions. These are:

1 Why's of causal explanation: these are to do with the
   efficient and final causes which account for natural and
   mechanical phenomena
2 Why's of motivation: these require an explanation of actions
   or psychological states
3 Why's of logical justification: why's which refer to habitual
   orderings and rules

Questions not in the 'why' form are classified according to the
topics they refer to, for example, questions of causal explanation
and questions relating to human actions and intentions. This
classification only partially coincides with that for 'why'.

Underlying this study of Piaget's is the idea that the child's
'why's' initially arise from faulty assumptions about the world.
The child believes that everything has a cause, and that motivations
can be imputed to objects, etc. Why's are believed to decrease
overall as egocentrism decreases, and the child makes more use of
observation of events and relationships, rather than imputing to
them intentions based on an animistic understanding of the universe.
Why's are seen as arising from precausal thought; in other words,
from some kind of faulty thinking.

This implicit assumption is challenged by Nathan Isaacs (21) in
his study of children's 'why' questions, based on examples of 'why'
questions asked by children at The Maltings school. Isaacs distinguishes five main functions of 'why' questions:

1 'Why' denoting 'Epistemic puzzlement', that is, 'why's
   triggered off by a sudden disparity between past experiences
   and a present event
2 'Why' as inquiry about motives, uses, intentions, purposes,
   functions. These are demands for familiar classes of information arising out of simple ignorance
3 'Why's' of causal intervention, control, deduction, selection
   or analysis. Here, the real interest is an explanation
4 'Why' as a demand for logical justification. These are addressed to beliefs and statements which strike the child as
   anomalous
5 'Why's' which are not questions, but expanations expressing
   anger, surprise, disbelief, etc.

Of these, the main opposition to Piaget's work is derived from the
why's of 'Epistemic Puzzlement'. Isaacs sees these as deriving not
from any defect in the child's thought which passes with age, but,
on the contrary, as deriving from the successful functioning of the

child's cognitive organisation. Questions like 'Why doesn't the ink run out when you hold up a fountain pen?', 'Why don't we see two things with our two eyes?', 'Why don't we milk pigs?' are seen by Isaacs as arising from the child's puzzlement because some phenomenon he observes does not 'fit' with rules and regularities which the child has constructed on the basis of previous experience. 'In this sense, 'why' means open-minded puzzlement, and demand for any sort of help which will actually help to put one to right.'

Isaacs sees this 'Epistemic Puzzlement' as an example of the similarity of the child's thought to our own, rather than as immature thinking whose structure alters with age and experience.

> Intelligent and inquiring grown-ups ask the same type of questions every day. Some of the most important and fruitful scientific inquiries set out from just such starting points. They are typical beginnings of new and better integrative knowledge. They initiate revision, reorganisation, and new, previously unthought of lines of extension of knowledge.

Thus for Isaacs, the child's epistemic why's represent some of his most significant learning situations; they are indications that he is actively interested in his knowledge as such and directly concerned with whether it is (a) correct, (b) sufficient, and (c) clear and unambiguous.

We have noted that both these studies place a heavy emphasis on 'why' questions, in line with what seems to be a generally shared belief that 'wh- questions', and of these, the why's especially, are somehow more useful than yes-no questions. In their recent study of answering behaviours of mothers and children, Robinson and Rackstraw (22) go so far as to exclude non-wh- questions from their analysis altogether. They divide questions up into open-ended and closed questions. Open-ended questions are defined as being equivalent to 'wh- questions', in response to which 'the answerer has to supply new lexical items whose characteristics will depend upon the particular interrogative word used'. Closed questions are defined as being equivalent to 'yes-no' questions; that is, they are marked by the predicator preceding the subject, or by question intonation being applied to a declarative sentence.

> As these questions may always be, and frequently are answered by a simple 'Yes' or 'No', the answers are so constrained as to be of little linguistic interest ... No new lexical items are required in reply to closed questions.

We see the relationship between wh- questions and yes-no questions as being rather more complex than this. Wh- questions are not necessarily open-ended in terms of the answer they require; and they may be constructed not from gaps in a conceptual framework, but from the lack of a conceptual framework at all. Similarly, yes-no questions do not necessarily close down allowable replies to simple affirmation or negation; and they may be evidence of successful cognitive functioning, in that the framing of a yes-no question may require more information and structuring on the part of the questioner than does a wh- question. This view is expressed by Cazden, (23) but unfortunately, she does not present any evidence to support it.

> In the search for knowledge, yes-no questions and wh- questions place different cognitive burdens on the speaker and the

listener ... Yes-no questions and wh- questions are often called
'general' and 'specific' questions respectively, but these labels
seem appropriate only when applied to the expected answer. If
one considers the knowledge required on the part of the speaker,
the labels might better be reversed. In other words, with yes-no
questions, the cognitive burden falls on the speaker (which is
why teachers are admonished to avoid them); with wh- questions,
the burden falls on the listener.

An example of a yes-no question comes from a group talking about a
science task concerned with work and energy.

David:	Is there, is there any, any energy used when you let a wheel go down a hill?
Barbara:	Yes
Marianne:	Yeah, because you need, energy to push it off, don't you?
Bill:	Yeah
David:	Well, you're not, you're not pushing it off, are you, you're just letting it go?

It may be true formally that to reply either 'Yes' or 'No' to these
questions would constitute an answer. It is quite clear from looking at these questions in context, however, that such an answer
would be completely inadequate to the social demands of group talk.
In this case the yes-no form of the question requires the respondent
to commit himself to Yes or No, but its context in problem-solving
discussion makes it function also as a demand for the respondent to
go on beyond the terms offered by the question and to construct supporting propositions. We might ask ourselves how we would have
understood the exchange if it had ended after Barbara's reply of
'Yes'. This would seem like a rejection of the whole of David's
lead: in such a discussion as this the extension of an answer
beyond yes or no may operate as an indication of willingness to collaborate in a particular strategy.

The strategy in question seems to be the construction, evaluation, and modification of alternative possibilities. We can see
here a direct continuity between the functions of questioning in the
young child as described by Lewis and Isaacs and the purposes which
they serve for the older children in discussions.

There are two main sources of discontinuity between questioning
in group discussion, and questioning as it has been described by
other workers, Lewis and Isaacs apart. These are: (a) that, in
common with Lewis and Isaacs, we see questioning to operate not only
to bring about closure of an information gap, but more importantly,
to create new structures and new understandings; and (b) that we do
not see any necessary correlation between the form in which a
question is posed and its cognitive power. We believe that these
two points are closely connected. What the members of our groups
gained in understanding from the exchange of questions and answers
seemed to relate not directly to the form of the questions but - as
would be expected - to the interpretation placed upon them. This in
turn would partly depend upon social relationships within the group.

We have described in earlier chapters the processes by which the
children collaborate in the creation of new understanding. Much of
this joint construction goes on by invitations to other group
members to contribute; often (but not always) such invitations are

posed in the form of questions. (24) The particular question form
does not seem to matter. In the example we quoted above, to reply
merely with 'yes' or 'no' simply because of the form in which a
question was posed, would have been to opt out of the expected
social relationships in that situation. To do so would have amount-
ed to redefining the situation from one where members jointly shaped
their own learning, to one where a group member reserved the right
to monitor and structure the learning process, as, for example, a
teacher might. In effect, he would arbitrarily decide to refuse the
'invitation to construct' which is implicit in the question, in
favour of a pedantic response to surface formal features alone.
     In practice, children in our groups rarely refuse the 'invitation
to construct'; this means that the cognitive gains from 'yes-no'
questions can be just as high as those from so-called 'open'
questions, because both can and do lead to exploration and to re-
structuring. Thus, children in these groups, when asked questions
which some workers would describe as 'closed', reply by extension
and elaboration along lines that have not been specifically asked
for, and the appropriateness of their replies are borne out by the
responses of those who asked the questions. In so far as this occurred, we believe that it occurred in response to the children's
view of their social situation, and in the following final section,
we want to explore the differences between this group work as a
social context and certain other contexts in which questioning has
been studied.

3 QUESTIONING AND SOCIAL POWER

Evidence from various other studies suggests that social factors may
be important influences on the ways questions are used and responded
to. Coulthard and Ashby, (25) for instance, in their study of
doctor-patient interviews, describe how doctors maintain tight
control over the progress of the interviews and particularly over
the giving of information by patients. Typically, the doctor begins
the interview with an open question about what is troubling the
patient. Coulthard and Ashby note that although this opening potentially offers the patient the opportunity to give a fairly
lengthy description of his troubles, only 2 out of the 24 patients
they studied actually did reply at any length. The rest gave only
short replies, and waited for the doctor to question them further.
In the light of the analysis offered by Coulthard and Ashby we can
see why this should be. Doctors interrupt patients when they give
information which has not been specifically asked for, and control
the interaction so as to obtain the information they do want, even
if the patient is unwilling to give it. Patients are aware that the
doctor because of his specialist knowledge is interpreting what they
say in the light of a frame of reference not available to them.
Most therefore supply initial information and wait for the doctor to
lead them to the information which is relevant within HIS frame.
Some may even have experienced brusque interruption in the course of
previous interviews with a doctor. Thus, whether a question which
has an 'open' form will be construed as open or closed depends on
the relative allocation of authority to questioner and answerer.

Teachers similarly control the discourse that goes on in their lessons. Sinclair and Coulthard (26) and Martin Hammersley, (27) amongst others, have described how teachers' questions serve to maintain social control of classes as well as to further pedagogic aims. Most questions asked by teachers are 'exam questions' in Searle's (28) sense: that is, they are questions to which the teacher already knows the answer. The pupil is required to demonstrate that he can supply that predetermined answer. It is the teacher who decides what constitutes a relevant and acceptable answer, and who can choose to reject altogether any answers which he judges to fall outside the implicit frame of reference in which he is working. As Hammersley points out,

> the teacher's framing of his questions and his treatment of pupil answers and initiatives are lesson-planning decisions - decisions about ... what the topic is, what points will be made, in what order and detail, with what slant, in order to carry on from and lead on to what, etc.

The function of such questions for the pupils - unlike that of the questions asked in our groups - is not to invite the construction of understanding but to test whether pupils are operating within the teacher's Content Frame. Accepting this Frame is not just a matter of 'understanding' but of conceding the teacher's authority, of accepting his Interaction Frame too. Each pupil has to guide his replies by intuiting the criteria of relevance which constitute the teacher's Content Frame.

A study of questioning behaviour in Hawaiian classrooms gives some indication of how this may affect children's participation in lessons. (We are aware, however, that it is not appropriate to extrapolate freely from this Hawaiian study to British classrooms since the relationship is likely to be further complicated by cultural differences.) Stephen Boggs (29) describes how, in response to a teacher's question, perhaps a dozen children put up their hands and of these several shouted out the answer without being named, whereas children who were named by the teacher either failed to reply or gave only a minimal reply, in spite of having put up their hands. After further participant study Boggs concluded that these children volunteered most information to a receptive adult who was not asking questions, or to an adult who asked the whole group rather than naming individuals. Attempts at conversation between adult and children in which the adult continually asked questions obtained very little response from the children, whereas amongst the children questions were asked and answered volubly. Boggs presumed that the children were responding (a) to the adult's superior authority compared with the more equal relationship with other children, and (b) to the dyadic relationship when a child is named by the teacher as compared with the collective relationship between the children.

It is just such a collective relationship that we observed in our small group discussions. Members were free to shift the topic, to try out new formulations and to explore alternatives, since none of the questions asked concealed positional claims to impose a frame on the discussion - to guide its direction or to judge the relevance of answers. The members of our groups cast their bread upon the waters. They were each others' resources and most of their utter-

ances were contributions to thinking. Their occasional questions
did not seek to control but to invite; this is why they did not
fall into easily recognisable functional categories, as do many of
a teacher's utterances. Their questions were at the respondents'
disposal, to utilise as they would.

It has become clear to us in the course of this study that the
allocation of power affects how people take part in the formulating
of knowledge. The effect of placing control of relevance in the
hands of one person is to emphasise his content frame, and this will
affect profoundly the basis upon which others participate. If on
the other hand alternative frames are open to negotiation this will
influence not only who takes part but also the knowledge which is
celebrated. Thus, what is learnt by discussion in a group of peers
will be different in kind as well as content from what is learnt
from teachers. When the criteria of relevance are negotiated and
not imposed, the Content Frames which participants develop in the
course of the negotiation are likely to bear more directly upon the
learner's actions since they will be idiomatically related to the
frames through which he is currently interpreting the world about
him. As we pointed out in the previous chapter, the very indeterminacy of the frames negotiated in our groups was a condition of their
developing new understandings: the members of the groups were able
to explore alternative meanings rather than to rehearse an established Content Frame taken over from a teacher.

It would be easy for an unsympathetic reader to dismiss such
learning contemptuously as likely to be vague, unselfcritical or
downright wrong. Although we were often impressed by the quality
of children's discussion, it is true that at times its quality was
less satisfactory. Of course, not all the lessons carefully
structured by teachers result in well-shaped or accurate learning;
,we must beware of contrasting small group talk with an idealised
version of class-teaching. But we are not claiming that all educational purposes can be carried out in small groups; that would
be absurd. Our study has made it clear that younger adolescents of
average I.Q. can under helpful circumstances carry out collaborative
learning in small groups, and that at times they display impressive
cognitive and social abilities. Our point is that to place responsibility in the learners' hands changes the nature of that
learning by requiring them to negotiate their own criteria of relevance and truth. If schooling is to prepare young people for responsible adult life, such learning has an important place in the
repertoire of social relationships which teachers have at their
disposal.

THE TASKS

THE PEARL

In the Introduction to 'The Pearl', John Steinbeck says that the
story may be a parable and that, 'perhaps everyone takes his own
meaning from it'.

Discuss among yourselves what you have found in the story so far –
the 'good and bad things, and black and white things and good and
evil things' as Steinbeck says; and any points about the characters, the setting, the way the book is written, that you feel worth
discussing.

PROBLEMS OF NATIONAL PARKS

National Parks provide:

    (a) Mountains, lakes, open country, waterfalls and farming
        land.
    (b) National Parks accommodate climbing, ski-ing, fell walking,
        camping, sailing and swimming.
    (c) People are demanding roads, camping sites, caravan sites,
        hotels, car parks, restaurants, refreshment stalls, kiosks,
        toilets, swimming pools, petrol stations, garages, tennis
        courts, cinemas, night clubs and casinos.

How can these demands be met without spoiling the natural beauty and
attractions?

CAUSES OF VANDALISM

An interview with 'Ron'

    A Yes, from then on I went with the Boys. I'd play dice and
       billiards with them, play the juke-boxes, picking up jobs.
       That went on till the middle of last year, when I thought all
       this was getting me nowhere.

The Boys? Well, our clique we could be about 100, 150.
Once we went over to the East End, there were 200 of us in
cars and lorries and vans; we went to fight against the
Greeks and the Turkish down in the Commercial Road. There was
a terrific punch-up. Only a few people got pulled in.

Ordinary way, of course, there weren't so many. Our clique
we'd meet in billiards halls, we'd play dice. For instance we
might go to the Greek Caff and play the juke-box, me and a few
mates, and one of us might say, 'Let's go over to Camberwell
and have a punch-up.' So we'd go to a caff down that way, and
one of us would say, 'Anyone here thinks he's a hard nut?' and
then we'd bring out the Boys and there'd be a fight. Or else
we'd try to get somebody out of a dance hall. We used to
stand and look for a bit of bother, you know, someone'd look
at us cheeky and we'd get him outside.

Q   What about the fighting - how did you set about it?
A   Well, it'd start with fists like, and then somebody'd get
    rough. We used bottles and chains and hammers... or we'd try
    to fight the Blacks. We used to shout at them in the street,
    'You black bastards', to try to provoke them, to beat them up,
    like. Over Brixton way, we'd try to stop them getting off
    buses, to frighten them. We'd often go for the Blacks, we
    don't like them round here, we hate them.
Q   Did you yourself like fighting?
A   Ever since I was a little kid I wanted to make people be
    frightened of me... All along I had the ambition to be
    somebody. I never had the chance to be somebody...

(This interview was first published in T.R.Fyvel, 'Insecure
Offenders', Chatto & Windus, 1961; the extract used here is
taken from R.H.Poole and P.J.Shepherd (eds), 'Impact', book 2,
'Themes and Topics', Heinemann, 1967.)

What do you think this interview tells you about the causes of
vandalism?
Do you think that Ron's last comment is particularly relevant?

WORK/ENERGY

We use the idea of WORK as a measure of how much ENERGY changes from
one form to another.

WORK is done when a force moves.

Here are some energy changes. Discuss them, and work out the ones
in which work is done:

  (a) Electricity to light in a light bulb
  (b) Heat to movement in a steam engine
  (c) Food to movement on a bicycle

Think of any other energy changes.

Is work always done when energy changes form?

STEVE'S LETTER OF NOTICE

Dear Sir,
You must think I'm crazy trying this one on me. Telling me it
was a nice interesting job for the holidays. Just light work!
I don't see YOU getting down on your knees on a concrete floor,
not likely! AND they keep spitting and throwing down ice creams
and fag ends all mixed together, it makes you sick. You must
think I'm crazy.
   Next time you want someone to do your dirty work you want to
choose someone who's daft. I wouldn't be seen dead in the place.
Not at that money. And that Sam in the kitchen with his jokes.
You can keep it.

Yours faithfully,
Steve

Steve wrote this letter giving notice that he was leaving after
spending the summer holidays working in a café. But after he'd
written it, he remembered that summer jobs are hard to come by and
that he might need a job there again next holidays. How do you
think he should alter, or rewrite it, if he wants to be employed in
the same café again?

CARBON DIOXIDE IN WATER

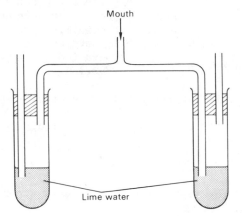

One person take the tube M. in your mouth and breathe in and out
through your mouth until a change takes place in the lime water.

Q. Why does the apparatus only let air in through one tube and
    only let the air out through the other?
    LOOK AT THE ARRANGEMENT OF THE TUBES.
Q. Does the lime water change most in the 'in' tube or the 'out'
    tube?
Q. How is air that you breathe out different from air that you
    breathe in?

YOU WILL HAVE TO REMEMBER WHICH GAS IT IS THAT CAUSES THE CHANGE
IN LIME WATER.

'DISCUSSIONS' TASK

Sometimes discussions seem to work very well, and sometimes they
don't seem to get off the ground. This happens in all discussions.
We're trying to find out what helps make good discussions.

You're going to listen to a tape of yourselves talking about 'The
Pearl'. When you have listened to it, we'd like you to talk about
it. We want to hear your ideas about what things help to make
useful discussions.

Here are some questions that might help.

 1 Which bits of the discussion went best? What kind of things
    seemed to help? What did people say that got the discussion
    moving?
 2 When did the discussion come up against dead ends? Can you
    tell what caused this?
 3 Have you learnt anything from hearing yourselves that will
    help you in tackling future discussions?
 4 Do you think that discussing in a group is as useful as work-
    ing on your own?
    Is it as useful as working in full class with the teacher?

LIFE IN THE TRENCHES

Discuss among yourselves life in the trenches during the First World
War.

What was it like?

What sort of discomforts and dangers did the soldiers face?

What would you dislike most if you found yourself in a similar situation? The danger or the discomfort?

BIRD'S EGGS

 1 Chip a small hole in the blunt end of the egg, and peep
    through it. What is there at this end of the egg? Why is it
    there?
 2 Crack the egg into a dish, without breaking the yolk. Find a
    small white speck on the yolk. What do you think this is?
 3 External fertilisation is the method of reproduction used by
    frogs and fish. Do you think a bird's egg could be fertilised
    inside the hen's body? What makes you think so?
 4 Will it be fertilised before the shell is put on, or after?
 5 The mother hen turns her eggs occasionally? Why?
 6 Look for coiled white strings in the egg white which attach
    the yolk to the shell. What are they there for?

SPACEMAN

We placed a corked bottle under a bell jar.

We pumped the air out of the bell jar with a vacuum pump.

Then the cork came out.

    1   Discuss among yourselves the relationship between the pressure
        in the **BOTTLE** and the pressure under the **BELL JAR** when all the
        air had been sucked out.
    2   Why did the cork come out?
    3   If a piece of rock hit a space ship and made a hole in it,
        what would happen to the air inside?
    4   What would happen to the spaceman if he stepped out into space
        without a space suit on?

CAUSES OF GANG VIOLENCE

Some teenage boys join gangs, and spend a lot of their leisure time
fighting other gangs.

They don't only fight in self-defence, but sometimes make an excuse
to pick a fight.

They may start off by only fighting with their fists, but sometimes,
someone gets rough, and they start using bottles, chains, or knives.

Why do you think boys fight in gangs like this?

NOTES

CHAPTER 1 THE CHILDREN AND THEIR TALK

1 Barnes, D., 'From Communication to Curriculum', Penguin, 1976.
2 Cronbach, L.J., 'Essentials of Psychological Testing', Harper & Row, Second Edition, 1960.
3 For a study which makes this assumption, see Turner, G.J. and Pickvance, R.E., Social Class Differences in the Expression of Uncertainty in Five-year-old Children, in Bernstein, B., 'Class, Codes and Control', vol.2, Routledge & Kegan Paul, 1969.
4 From the paper Towards a Sociological Semantics, in Halliday, M.A.K., 'Explorations in the Functions of Language', Edward Arnold, 1973.
5 See especially the diagram on p.101 of Halliday (1973), op.cit.
6 See Hasan, R., 'Grammatical Cohesion in Spoken and Written English', University College London and Longmans Green, 1968.
7 See for example Sinclair, J.M. and Coulthard, M., 'Towards an Analysis of Discourse: the English used by Teachers and Pupils', Oxford University Press, 1975.
8 C.f. Cicourel, A.V., Ethnomethodology, in 'Cognitive Sociology', Penguin, 1972.
9 Coombs, C.H., 'A Theory of Data', John Wiley, 1964.
10 Glaser, B. and Strauss, A., 'The Discovery of Grounded Theory', Aldine, 1967.
11 See Halliday, M.A.K., Language Structure and Language Function, in Lyons, J. (ed.), 'New Horizons in Linguistics', Penguin, 1970. For an example of the Prague approach see Danes, F., A Three-Level Approach to Syntax, in 'Travaux Linguistiques de Prague', 1, 1964.
12 Sinclair and Coulthard, 1975, op.cit.
13 Peel, E.A., 'The Nature of Adolescent Judgment', Staples, 1971.

CHAPTER 2 MAKING SENSE TOGETHER

1 The bracket indicates that all or part of these two utterances were simultaneous.

CHAPTER 3   STUDYING GROUP TALK

1   Watson, J. and Potter, R.J., An Analytic Unit for the Study of
    Interaction, 'Human Relations', vol.15, no.2, 1962.
2   An example of some issues generated by a particular set of
    recordings when discussed by a group of English teachers can be
    found in Barnes, D., Churley, P. and Thompson, C., Group Talk
    and Literary Response, 'English in Education', vol.5, no.3,
    1971.
3   This phrase is used by Eric Hoyle in Strategies of Curriculum
    Change, in Watkins, A.R. (ed.), 'In Service Training: Structure
    and Content', Ward Lock, 1973.

CHAPTER 4   FRAMES: HOW TO UNDERSTAND CONVERSATIONS

1   'Indeterminacy' is used in a similar sense by R.Walker and
    C.Adelman in 'Towards a Sociography of Classrooms', Centre for
    Science Education, Chelsea College of Science and Technology,
    1972.
2   Garfinkel, H., Remarks on Ethnomethodology, in Gumperz, J.J. and
    Hymes, D. (eds), 'Directions in Sociolinguistics', Holt,
    Rinehart & Winston, 1972.
3   Schutz, A., 'The Phenomenology of the Social World', Heinemann,
    1932, p.52: 'Only from the point of view of the reflective
    glance do there exist discrete experiences. Only the already
    experienced is meaningful, not that which is being experienced.'
4   See for example, Miller, G.A., The Magic Number Seven Plus or
    Minus Two: some limits on our capacity for processing infor-
    mation, 'Psychol. Review', vol.63, 1956, pp.81-96; Gibson,
    J.J., 'The Senses considered as Perceptual Systems', Allen &
    Unwin, 1968; Broadbent, D.E., 'Perception and Communication',
    Pergamon Press, 1958.
5   'Frame' here derives from 'frame of reference'; it is not
    related to B.Bernstein's use of the term in On the Classifi-
    cation and Framing of Educational Knowledge, in Bernstein, B.,
    'Class, Codes and Control', vol.1, Routledge & Kegan Paul, 1971,
    nor to the concept used in Goffman, E., 'Frame Analysis',
    Penguin, 1975.
6   See, for example, Hoetker, J. and Ahlbrand, W.P., The Per-
    sistence of the Recitation, 'Am.Educ.Res.Journ.', vol.6, no.2,
    1969, p.145; Bellack, A.A. et al., 'The Language of the
    Classroom', Teachers College Press, 1966; de Landsheere, G.,
    'Comment les Maitres Enseignent', Ministère de l'Education
    Nationale et de la Culture, Brussels, undated; Barnes, D.,
    Britton, J. and Rosen, H., 'Language, the Learner and the
    School', Penguin, 1971.
7   Our analysis of the marshalling of knowledge for the interpret-
    ing of conversation owes a debt to Rommetveit, R., Linguistic
    and Non-linguistic Components of Communication, in Moscovici, S.
    (ed.), 'The Psychosociology of Language', Markham, 1972. Our
    'content frame' has something in common with Rommetveit's
    'cognitive representation', though the latter is treated as if
    it were static.

8 Our use of the term 'gatekeeper' is derived from William Fawcett
   Hill's 'Learning Thru Discussion', Sage Publications, 1969.
9 A Schutz, 1932, op.cit. adopts Husserl's strategy of attributing
   an 'ideal objectivity' of meaning to each utterance, irre-
   spective of any person who understands it. We can see nothing
   to be gained by this idealised construction.

CHAPTER 5 QUESTIONS AND QUESTIONING

1 Jespersen, U.O.H., 'A Modern English Grammar', vol.4, Allen &
   Unwin, 1946.
2 For example, Zandvoort, R.W., 'A Handbook of English Grammar',
   Longman, 1957, and Kruisinga, E., 'Handbook of Present Day
   English', Kemink (Utrecht), 1932.
3 O'Connor, J.D. and Arnold, G.F., 'Intonation of Colloquial
   English', Longman, 1961.
4 Bolinger, D.L., 'Interrogative Structures of American English',
   University of Alabama Press, 1957.
5 Huddleston, R.D., 'The Sentence in Written English', Cambridge
   University Press, 1971.
6 Austin, J.L., 'How to Do Things With Words', Oxford University
   Press, 1962.
7 Searle, J.R., 'Speech Acts', Cambridge University Press, 1969.
8 Quirk, R. and Greenbaum, S., 'A University Grammar of English',
   Longman, 1974.
9 Crystal, D., 'Prosodic Systems and Intonation in English',
   Cambridge University Press, 1969.
10 O'Connor and Arnold, 1961, op.cit.
11 Harrah, D., 'Communication: A Logical Model', M.I.T. Press,
   Massachusetts, 1963.
12 Waisman, F., 'The Principles of Linguistic Philosophy',
   Macmillan, 1965.
13 Harrah, 1963, op.cit. summing up the position of Wittgenstein
   and Hamblin.
14 Berlyne, D.E. and Frommer, F.D., Some Determinants of the
   Incidence and Content of Children's Questions, 'Child Development', vol.37, 1966, pp.177-89. Piaget, J., 'The Language and
   Thought of the Child', Routledge & Kegan Paul, 1960 (First
   published 1928). Robinson, W.P. and Rackstraw, S.J., 'A
   Question of Answers', Routledge & Kegan Paul, 1972.
15 Cazden, C.B., Children's Questions: their Forms, Functions, and
   Roles in Education, in W.W.Hartup (ed.), 'The Young Child',
   vol.2, National Association for the Education of Young Children,
   Washington, 1972.
16 Ross, H., Forms of Exploratory Behaviour in Young Children, in
   B.Foss (ed.), 'New Perspectives in Child Development', Penguin,
   1974.
17 Ross, ibid.
18 Lewis, H.H., 'Language, Thought and Personality in Infancy and
   Childhood', Harrap (London) and Basic Books (New York), 1963.
19 Hall, G.S., 'Aspects of Child Life and Education', Ginn, 1907.
20 Piaget, J., 1960, op.cit.
21 Isaacs, N. Children's 'Why' Questions, in 'Intellectual Growth
   in Young Children', by Susan Isaacs, Routledge, 1930.

22 Robinson, W.P. and Rackstraw, S., 1972, op.cit.
23 Cazden, C.B., 'Child Language and Education', Holt Rinehart & Winston, 1972.
24 Just under 25 per cent of all the utterances made in the discussions we recorded were in question form.
25 Coulthard, M. and Ashby, M., Talking with the Doctor, 'Journal of Communication', Summer, 1975.
26 Sinclair and Coulthard, 1975, op.cit.
27 Hammersley, M., The Organisation of Pupil Participation, 'Sociological Review', August, 1974.
28 Searle, J.R., 'Speech Acts', Cambridge University Press, 1969.
29 Boggs, S., The Meaning of Questions and Narratives to Hawaiian Children, in Cazden, C.B., John, V.P. and Hymes, D. (eds), 'Functions of Language in the Classroom', Teachers College Press, 1972.

NAME INDEX

SUBJECT INDEX

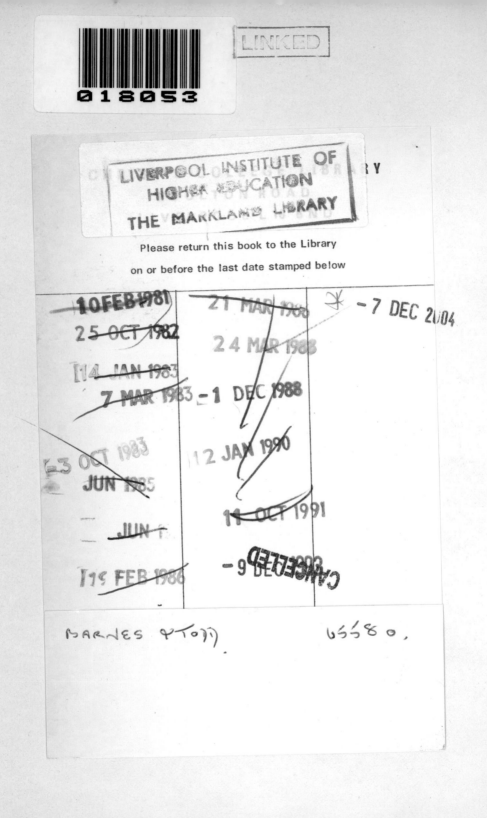